T0366271

GOOD NEWS

THE PASSION, DEATH AND RESURRECTION OF JESUS, THE CHRIST

BY

PETER J. RIGA

authorHOUSE®

AuthorHouse™
1663 Liberty Drive
Bloomington, IN 47403
www.authorhouse.com
Phone: 1-800-839-8640

Published by AuthorHouse 7/19/2013

ISBN: 978-1-4817-7895-4 (sc)
ISBN: 978-1-4817-7896-1 (e)

Library of Congress Control Number: 2013912778

INTRODUCTION

For many years I have wanted to write a book about the passion, death and resurrection of Jesus. I have from time to time written essays on the passion and death of Jesus but only now have I been able to put them together in one book.

There is never enough we can say about this heart of our faith. Without the resurrection of Jesus, the Christian faith would not be faith at all. It would be simply the moral doctrine of a great religious leader who lived and died like every other religious founder. We could appreciate the grandeur of his thought and admire the integrity of his person. But Jesus would have been no different from the others with their legacies and memories that could be read and imitated down through the ages but nothing really extraordinary.

But Christianity from the very beginning held to something radically different about this Jesus who is the Christ: that he died under the authority of the Roman procurator Pontius Pilate, that he was buried in a tomb like every other dead man but that death was overcome in him when he rose from the dead. Not just in memory and as a memorial in the hearts and minds of his followers; but that it was the same Jesus who walked the hills of Palestine, the same Jesus who talked, ate and taught his disciples for three years; the same Jesus it was who rose from the dead by the power of God, thereby overcoming death once and for all into the new power of God. Jesus is the beginning of the new creation.

Hard to believe precisely because it is such good news. It is good news because an anxiety over our end and the end of those we hold near and dear has been overcome through this unique person of Jesus, the Christ. Now that is the heart of the good news, of the Christian message that has come down to us after two thousand years. No other religious leader could make such a claim and it is the central truth which must be held under pain of complete failure and deception ever to

1

be delivered to men and women of our world. Without this core message, we Christians are the most miserable of human beings because then death would still hold us captive and the grave the final answer too all of man's dreams, desires and aspirations.

But no! Christ is risen and we who believe that are risen with him. That message is indeed good news which if true, changes everything. Our whole world and its outlook is changed, our whole outlook of life is different, optimistic even in the midst of whatever life brings us.

I have divided this good news into three sections.

Section one deals with the events leading up to the resurrection, the suffering and passion of Jesus.

Section two deals with the resurrection of Christ culminating in Pentecost and the sending of the Spirit to form the body of Christ which is the Church.

Section three deals with implications of the resurrection of Jesus: his royalty, the new commandment, the meaning of redemption in Jesus, the believer and not seeing, etc.

All this constitutes a very small book but with a lot of room for meditation and reflection on these central events of the Christian message. As I have said, no book, no library could ever contain all the implications of this central pascal mystery of Christianity. The only thing I have hoped to do is to give some fresh insights into this central event so that you, the reader, may appreciate and love this truly good news of our joy and salvation. If I shall have accomplished so much, I shall have been richly rewarded for my effort, truly humble as it is. I ask only that ifI shall succeed in this effort, that you remember me before the altar of God.

Houston, Texas
The Holy Year of Salvation
July 1, 2013

TABLE OF CONTENTS

SECTION I

THE PASSION AND SUFFERING OF JESUS

CHAPTER I
PALM SUNDAY

This day is a day of memory of the recital of the passion of Christ. It is important that at the beginning of the high holy days, we bring to mind some basic Christian truths.

MURDER: God is totally innocent of the cross. The execution of Christ is a crime disguised as an act of justice. "He whom you have crucified (Jesus)" repeats Saint Peter in the *Acts of the Apostles.* This crime recapitulates all the murders committed in humanity "from the blood of the innocent Abel" *(Matthew 23:35).* Easter reveals to us all the crosses that we have prepared and perpetrated everywhere in spite of God, against his word. We participate in on going murder each time that we despise others, each time that we ignore others, each time we abuse others, each time we mistreat and lie to others or treat them as nothing *(Matthew 5:21-22).* That is why the passion of Christ concerns us intimately because the cross is not some sort of spectacle which we view from the outside. We are at the scene- each of us- with the disciples who flee the drama of a man who was their friend and now become a stranger for them: "I do not know the man" Peter repeats three times *(Matthew 26: 26, 72 and 74).* To show that the whole world participated in putting Jesus to death, the Evangelists turn the condemnation of Jesus into a judicial process, both a Jewish and a pagan trial. Jew and pagan represent in the Bible enemy brothers *sharing all humanity.* It matters little that it was not a true judicial proceeding. What it tells us is that enemy brothers worked together to commit murder. Everyone, Jew and pagan, commits murder.

PARDON: All the Gospels hold that it is the will of God that Christ endures the cross. How shall we understand that? In this way: God wants to assume and go beyond our evil and our misfortune. God comes in and by Christ and puts himself in the place of all our victims. This means that every evil done to man attains God himself ("it is to me that you have done it" *Matthew 25:40)* when Jesus freely and lovingly accepts his passion. What appears strikingly in this acceptance is *love* and it is precisely for that reason that Jesus during his passion, continues to call God "Father." To speak of the cross in terms of sacrifice, ransom to be paid risks missing what is happening here.

the revelation of God as love who goes so far as absolute pardon. The resurrection of Christ brings the process to an end and makes the "body of sin" disappear, the body of the just one who was killed. The Gospel is a sentence of acquittal. We are all pardoned if we begin to forgive and to love. If

GOD WITH US: Joining us at the very core of our distress, even into all of our hells, the hells that we have created and those created for us, God reveals himself "God with us" in every hell, every pain, even to the very end. This is just another way of saying "love." There is no disaster so great in our lives when we can say, "God is not there." He is *now* because he has been there *before*. No matter how much we have strayed or fallen or sunk, God is there with us. He is nourishment and drink unto eternal life. He is even there by us by means of us. Assimilated to Christ because he has assimilated himself to us, all have died in him; all our deaths become his death. Death no longer has power over him nor over us because we too can use that suffering-death to make love grows and shine forth. The cross is there to make us understand that our confidence continues to be valid, to be justified precisely because there where it seemingly is destroyed by those terrible events of Good Friday. If our confidence is not valid there, it is not valid at all. In meditating on the passion of Christ, it is not so much asked of us that we be sad or to afflict ourselves but to become ever more conscious of this love by which we are loved on that cross. Christ has not come to take away our pain or even to let us understand it; he has come forever to share it with us. The cross is glorious and already contains the germ or seed of the resurrection. It is scandal to the world but to those who believe, we are forgiven and shown love thereby, it is salvation. The cross is the foolishness of God becomes the wisdom of God. It is scandal to the Greeks and a stumbling block to the Jews but to us salvation and the wisdom of God (I *Corinthians 1:21-25).*

7

II

To understand the importance of this event of Palm Sunday we must remember all the activity of Jesus in Galilee far from the capitol where everything would be decided. Jesus announced the coming of the kingdom which many imagined would be a triumphal one to set matters aright and justice assured between peoples and individuals. From chapter ten in *Mark*, Jesus begins the long journey toward Jerusalem and the pascal mystery. Will the good news of the coming of the kingdom be ready and announced now? Didn't Jesus perform powerful signs and miracles which showed that in him there was an extraordinary power, that of God himself?

But everyone seems to forget that Jesus never performed a sign for himself or to acquire prestige and honor but only in favor of others and above all in *Mark*, he forbids all publicity about his actions. His entrance into Jerusalem revolves around the signs of ambiguity. First the disciples misunderstand the meaning of these events. There is also ambiguity in the signs themselves. Jesus makes a royal entry but on the fold of an ass, a humble animal of service and not on a horse which is an animal of nobility and war. A new born donkey is the kind of a kingdom and royalty which Jesus inaugurates. The image of God which Jesus gives is radically transformed and even reversed. The image of God of Jesus is one of service and gift because God is, essentially, love. Jesus is servant, gift, humiliated, crucified, humbled before men because his royal kingdom is that of love. Jesus radically changes the image of God from that of his contemporaries.

Each time that we say that we cannot believe in a God that permits Auschwitz or the death and suffering of little children, we are one with the logic of the disciples of Jesus who follow Jesus thinking he would establish a new worldly order. On the contrary, Jesus will subject himself to absolute disorder which the crucifixion represents. Certainly God is not absent from our violence, from torture and hunger, those of the street, of our wars, exclusions but he is there *in the role of our victims*. Christ recapitulates all these victims and contains them all; and Christ is no one else except God who is humiliated and mocked. But we cannot kill God who is life itself. The marvel is that recapitulated in Christ as victims, they are present at his passion as actors of murder but we are also and equally assumed in his resurrection. We therefore are those from one end to the other and it is that which we receive when we need or listen to the recital of the passion. We are not simply hearers but actors. It is in our lives that Jesus comes to take power over our death; it is there that the kingdom arrives. All this is memorialized in the Eucharist, this insuperable thanks to God for the gift of life which he has given in the midst of our death.

All through the passion, the evangelists - Mark in particular - draw our attention to the fact that Jesus is alone. Alone at Gethsemene where the disciples choose to sleep as they slept at the transfiguration. Alone at the moment of his arrest when all fled. No one can be next to Christ because we are all contained in him as all men were virtually contained in the first Adam. But alone on earth, Jesus is equally alone from heaven. The angels do not intervene, his Father remains silent. No one comes to his aid from the outside because all of the divine power resides in him which is as it were annihilated before the murderous will of men. Thus God manifests himself submissive and submitted to the projected designs of the liberty of men. *The secret of this way of being God is love.* Love to the very end, says John. God is with us everywhere we force him to go. Everything, heaven or earth, the divine and the human, inhabits the solitude of Christ. So too is it for us in all our trials and in all our deaths. We are always alone and yet we carry God and the world. Seemingly alone, we carry God and the whole world just as Christ, alone, carries us all.

CHAPTER II
THE HOLY TRIDUUM: THE COMING SCANDAL

Holy Thursday

When Jesus at supper takes water and begins to wash the feet of the disciples, they absolutely do not understand. Neither did they emotionally comprehend when he told them that he was going up to Jerusalem to be betrayed, beaten, put to death - too much for good Jews who anticipated the power and glory of the coming Messiah. One who would be humiliated, put to death and die? Impossible.

The same astonishment and mis-comprehension at the Last Supper when Jesus begins to wash their feet. In fact, the disciples are shocked. The fact that the Rabbi, the Master, the Lord on his knees before them to wash their feet is just unimaginable, totally contrary in the sociological context of the Greco-Roman and Semitic world of Jesus' day. The custom was for the host to have the feet of his guests washed by a non-Jewish slave, never by a close relative nor even by a freed slave.

Thus he who appears as the awaited Messiah, he who will come to establish the freedom of Israel, behaves not like a king but like a slave. We can clearly sympathize with Peter when he exclaims that Christ would never wash *his* feet.

Yet by this spectacular gesture, Jesus announced an even greater scandal to come: he who today freely chose "the condition of a slave" will die tomorrow as a thief between two malefactors. Jesus freely surrenders himself to the will and violence of man, who freely gives his life humiliated and beaten, without hatred and with forgiveness even for those who harmed him and who entrusted himself amidst the most abject humiliation and death, into the hands of his Father, into the night of death not knowing how or when the Father would answer.

All this is a complete reversal of worldly values already announced at Christmas: the unique Son of God chose to join our humanity, not by power of glory but by poverty. From this Holy

Thursday, the service of the brothers and sisters is no longer just a moral consequence of our faith in God. It is the very heart of our faith. To believe is to Love without measure both God and the brothers.

Good Friday: More Scandal

At the foot of the cross, all stops. It is as if the last page of the book has been turned, definitively turned. The future has no horizon. The stone is rolled in place over the tomb. It enclosed behind it the whole history of Jesus. There is nothing more to wait for.

Jesus enters the great silence. After having proclaimed the good news throughout Galilee, after having healed the sick, after opening the eyes of the blind and raising the dead, after having changed the hearts of the rich and the poor, Jesus goes to the very end of his love for men, for those whom his Father gave him. Jesus enters into the silence of death and his death means the absolute gift he made of his life to save each of the little ones which we are.

Everything is accomplished. Only the death on the cross can accomplish everything. Only his death can give force and meaning to his actions and to his words. The death of Jesus opens to a time of silence and of contemplation, the silence given us to understand his words. And it is precisely today that this word is complete, is accomplished. At the foot of the cross God speaks more strongly. The silence of Jesus in death reveals the face of the Father. At the foot of the cross all humanity is invited to enter into silence. The book is closed. The age of faith begins.

Easter Vigil: Life Within Our Tombs

Faithful to the end and beyond death, the women came with their spices and aromatic herbs. Women are always the first at the tomb, even today. They knew in their hearts and in their faith that death cannot enclose life, that death cannot kill love or fidelity. He is always living - he whom they carry in the warmth of their thoughts.

The women came to the tomb of Jesus, the rock was rolled back and the tomb empty. The women must run, they must sing. Lift up your eyes. He is risen, he is alive, he is living whom you seek and whom you love! They are the first witnesses of the resurrection, depository of the good news, first apostles of the risen one. Gone to bring that good news.

Christians are to cry with joy. If it was cold and somber in our hearts and lives, it is that storms have enclosed them from the warmth and light of the resurrection. Take away the stones, the tombs have been opened and life and light have flooded in.

Christ was dead, now he is alive, living. You were dead but Christ has given you life, has made you alive. Nailed to a cross, all your agonies have been burned away by the great fire of the resurrection. We are new men, living men. Cry, sing, light the candles. It is the feast of the one who lives, the call of life itself. It is the Easter of the Lord.

The Day of Easter: Faith and Joy

Everything begins anew. It is the first day of the week. The hour is still night but the dawn approaches. Mary Magdalene goes to the tomb; the day begins as she goes on her way. Darkness dissipates slowly. When she approaches the tomb she sees that the rock has been rolled back. Surprise and stupefaction: the tomb is empty. The body of Jesus is not there. We do not know where they have placed it. She rushes to tell the disciples.

It is a body she was seeking and not one who lives. For Mary Magdalene as for each of his disciples, they must cross the threshold of the empty tomb. Not just to see the status of the place and the absence of the body of Jesus but also to discover that the Word has been fulfilled to pass from darkness to the light. Up to that point, the disciples did not see, did not understand that according to Scripture, it was necessary for Jesus to rise form among the dead, to pass to a new life.

To pass to a new life, to come out of the darkness, to believe that our resurrection has already begun, behold that to which the resurrected one calls us. Let us not be afraid. At the threshold of the tomb God calls us to an act of faith. Let us dare together to pass over the empty tomb to welcome into our lives the light of Easter.

Let us pass through the empty tomb and say to our brothers and sisters that Christ is alive. Christ has risen!

CHAPTER III
HOLY THURSDAY

The Last Supper in each of the Gospels sums up the total message of Jesus. It gives meaning to all the events which are to transpire in the next few days. Christ gives in advance what men seek of him: his life. "This is my flesh, this is my blood" represents an act of freedom which assumes in advance the inevitable events which are being prepared for him. "No one takes my life except I give it" says Jesus (*John 10:18*). He gives his life as one gives bread to satisfy the hunger of the other. Thereby we learn that the fundamental nourishment of man which holds him in existence and life is God himself - that which we call God. "Nourishment that we do not know" (*John 4:32*) but whom Christ reveals to us. We draw our substance from God and already we suspect that the reality which sustains and establishes us, which is the very source of our being, is love. It should however be well understood that this word remains mysterious for us and that we are incapable of understanding all that it means.

The most common nourishment and drink in the countries of wheat and vines are bread and wine. They are every day nourishment but are charged with meaning: the relationship of man to nature which brings us forth, that exterior reality that we subsume interiorly to let us live. It is a relationship as well of each one of us to all others. Bread and wine are collective products but also subject of dispute and conflict (we can fight each other for bread). Gifts of the nourishing earth, but also the results of human technology and work which domesticate nature which itself is a sign of relation of men among themselves for better or for worse. Everything is there.

The acts of Jesus at the Last Supper take these elements to their ultimate meaning and go beyond them while not destroying their fundamental meaning but fulfilling them. Already the relationship between nourishment and the relationship to God was taken up in the Bible (*Genesis 1:29; 2:16-17; 9:3*). The remembrance of the manna in the desert goes along the same direction (*Exodus 16:1-18*) as the Last Supper. It is also central to the sixth chapter of *John* where Jesus declares himself the true bread given for the life of man.

Where the Synoptic Gospels speak of the body and blood of Christ, John substitutes the washing of the feet. That is, both recitals have the same meaning. "Do this in memory of me" is not only to reproduce his ritual gesture but also - and perhaps above all - to put oneself at the service of others. Thereby Jesus signifies that God is at the service of men, of their life and of their truth. "Do as I have done", "imitate" me is really to imitate God. To help men find and re-find their integrity the best way to "remember Christ" is to do charity. A charity of ourselves which goes all the way for the needs of others.

If we repeat the sacrament of Christ in ritual and in deed over and over again, it is because we have not yet arrived, we are not yet there. We are people along the way, on route to the promised land and as we go along we share the bread and wine along the route in ritual and in act.

CHAPTER IV
GOOD FRIDAY AND THE SUFFERING SERVANT

Saint John's view is that the passion of Jesus is his 'exaltation." Jesus is elevated above the earth so that the whole world can see him, "to look upon him" whom *we* have pierced. Without any doubt for John, the image of Christ elevated is an image of glory, a true elevation. Now is the time, says Jesus when he approached his passion, when the Son of Man is to be glorified (*John 12:23*). "Father, glorify the Son" (*John 17:1*). However, this glory is terribly paradoxical: it comes from the fact that the Son has been made sin for us (*II Corinthians 5:21*). In effect, John assimilates Jesus to the bronze serpent of *Numbers 21:4-9*. Israel in the desert was decimated by poisonous snakes - the exteriorization and materialization of an interior evil which infected the people: unbelief, doubt. On the order of God, Moses exposed an "elevated" bronze serpent on a pole which was pierced. All those who "looked upon it" were healed. In Chapter three John assimilates Jesus elevated from the earth to the serpent. Jesus thus becomes an image of our evil and of our distress. In *Isaiah 53*, the afflicted servant is offered before the eyes of all, and shows them his proper wounds for the people's sins. It is because Jesus is just, pure, that he can assimilate himself to the unjust and knows the result of evil doers, that he is glorified and receives a name which is above every name (*Philipians 2:9*).

"To look upon", "to turn towards", "to believe in" are all equivalent terms for John. The "look upon" is *first of all an admission*: we can't turn our heads away and make believe that we have not seen. We must look upon all the victims of our societies, of our politics, of our greed and selfishness. The media does not permit us to do otherwise with the pictures of those victims constantly before our eyes. They "elevate" these victims above the earth. We may deny it but we are all in solidarity with all those systems which sacrifice people for our own benefit (e.g. Nike).

In the admission of this "looking upon" there is the beginning of our healing and salvation. Brought along by our avowal, we arrive at the confidence in him who gave his life for us. For in Christ is shown an infinite love, a love who is God. The "looking upon" is at the same time a consciousness of crime and an acceptance of the sign of salvation. By that token, our confidence is displaced. Instead of looking to ourselves and our good works, we are brought to trust and have confidence in another, Jesus Christ. "Look toward" takes on the meaning of "going to" (*John 6:35*).

In the symbolism of John, the blood and water flowing from the side of Christ certainly refers to the Eucharist and Baptism which speak to us of a new birth, of a new creation. The exaltation of Christ is at the same time the exaltation of all men. The Spirit sent forth by the dying Christ who delivers the Spirit makes all things new. Baptism and the Eucharist are the signs of this new life, this new creation which permit us to rejoin the creative act of a humanity wed by God. *Thus we can receive the announcement of life exactly there where death does its work.* Christ rules from the cross.

Marvelous paradox.

II

Two thousand years after the event of Good Friday, we are still shocked that as Christians, we believe in a suffering and murdered God, murdered by the violence of men. The light of the world remains in the darkness of his own agony but confident in the goodness and mercy of his Father: "Eloi, Eloi, lama sabachthani" from *Psalm 22* as the prayer of a pious Jew abandoned by all except his absolute confidence in the goodness and mercy of God. It was a terrible shock to the early Christians as well as to us today, that the Son of God chose, willingly, the reality of a suffering and humiliated servant and not the power and dominance of the world. It was a pagan, the Roman centurion, who first confessed this. Irony and paradox

"Others he saved, himself he cannot save" was the taunt of his enemies even as he hung, nailed to a Roman gibbet and left to die in agony between two malefactors. In that one phrase, the evangelist tells us about the kind of power chosen by God for his Christ: his willingness to save others while never using his power for himself. His whole life, like his death, is one *for others*, never for himself. His mission was for others, to be a ransom for many, to give all that he had for his followers "even to the end." The phrase of the Gospel therefore should be read "others he saved *because* he did not want to save himself"; it was through his suffering servanthood that he delivers all he has for those whom he loved to the end. How little Christians have understood this complete non violence of Christ, his unwillingness to use worldly power to vindicate his love. Even today. He mounted that gibbet freely, and freely he appeals to all men to overcome their violence and hatred.

The tone was set the night before at the last meal he had with those whom he loved. He girds himself, gets on his knees and does something no self respecting Jew would ever do: he washes the feet of his disciples, and so he becomes a slave. That was to show his followers in what their

17

greatness and power would consist: to serve the brothers and sisters where the first shall be last and the last shall be first. Christ came as a servant out of love and the beaten, humiliated and nailed Christ to a cross would be the final testimonial of his love and his suffering servanthood. It is a lesson far too few Christians have ever understood so embedded are they with the power to dominate and to be first, "number one." The way of worldly power is so easy, so natural. That of Christ so unnatural.

On that cross, there were the two terrible scandals to Christians and non Christians alike: that the Christian God is one of humiliation and degradation on a Roman gibbet. And that refusing all power for himself ("do you not know Peter, that if I willed, the Father would give five legions of angels?"), remained alone, despised, dying in agony with only a prayer of confidence and trust in his Father. Some Christians console themselves by saying that being the Son of God, he knew that it was all temporary and that in three days he would rise. But did he? Because if he did, he would *not* be like us in all things except sin. *When we die, we die completely alone with only our loving confidence in the God who can raise the dead and make that which does not exist, to exist. We too die alone, in darkness but with confidence and trust in the living God.* And because he is the living God, God cannot ultimately die and must put death, to death. But how and when were unknown to Christ as it is unknown to us. And there is the second scandal of the Son of God: so much like us, the mystery of the incarnation was that he died with the same loving confidence as we.

"Eloi, Eloi, lama sabachthani" (*Psalm 22*).

Yet, we persist in calling today not 'terrible Friday' or 'black Friday' but 'Good Friday.' The promise and confidence of today will be revealed on the morrow, the grain that dies will produce much fruit. "I am the resurrection and the life." But today we do not know, we are in the darkness but with confidence and trust in the loving and living God.

18

CHAPTER V
THE AGONY AND SUFFERING OF JESUS

We are all made of death. The very act of living equals dying because everyday we live is a day we no longer have. Each day advances our death and we try to hide it or forget about it. When we are born, we are old enough to die. We are forced to see Good Friday in the light of Easter or as the affirmation of nonsense at the very edge of any meaning. We often forget the ordinary banality of Christ's death in communion with our pure and simple corruptibility.

Dead for our salvation, the Son of God died no less for us men, that is, by a simple sharing of our fleshly humanity. The death of Christ seen in the perspective of redemption can equally be seen in the horizon of his incarnation as "taking in the flesh" our own flesh and its most ordinary consequences. His flesh would have seen corruption, says Peter, if he had been abandoned in the place of the dead (*Acts 2:31*) just like everyone else.

In other words, everything happens as if the believer is always forced to co-perceive death in the interpretation of life or by spiritualizing death to the point of losing its biological consistence or by valorizing it by covering its evident nonsense (the absurdity of an existence necessarily condemned to its own disappearance). As soon as man comes to life (Bethlehem) he is old enough to die (Golgotha).

Christ had to die the same death as the rest of us - of our fathers and their fathers before them, of friends and relatives, of strangers and neighbors; and the death that all our loved ones will experience some day and we at the center of it all. The Son dies just as I will die, just as others died. It is uniquely to the weight given to death that the weight accorded to the resurrection is measured, to mine as well as that of Christ's.

To say of the Son of Man that he did not first suffer our own proper death is neither to respect

19

God, nor myself, nor my contemporaries. Not God because he himself deliberately lived at Gethsemene as on Golgotha, a particular agony of death; not myself because the exterior imposition of a meaning to my life as to my death often obscures the brightness of its nonsense. For us all, believer or not, the perspective of our own death undermines us in a double sense where it torments us and destroys us.

This agony of our finiteness and therefore, of our mortality is not sinful and that is why the Son assumed it in his proper humanity. For it is not from the power of man to die because he alone possesses so great an intense consciousness of death that it imposes on him an obligation to give meaning to his life. Everything does not reside in deciding for or against the meaning of life or theologically to opt for or against the sinful reason for our own death. The essential is to accept leaving that question in suspension neither despairing nor denying it by justification.

The Myth of the Golden Age

The believer often has difficulty in accepting mortality because he or she believes that it is derived from a form of original fall. Since man's creation was good in the eyes of God this does not mean that it was the most perfect possible. When God tells Adam that he will die the death (*Genesis 2:17*) this need not be a unilateral designation of biological death as such. In reality, it is not biological death which is the consequence of sin (the law of entropy is the law of the living) but it is the reverse, the refusal of this death, that is the non acceptance of our created finitude as such which is the cause of death.

As proof of this, consider the word of the serpent addressed to Eve in the garden. "You will be as gods" (*Genesis 3:5*). To desire to be immortal like the ancient mythologies, is this not to refuse the finiteness of our creation? The first man therefore did not have biological immortality. But

20

wanting immortality, like God, man rejects his creatureliness and dies the death. The myth of the golden age is there. With the incarnation of the Son of God, today we must try to show how that refusal of finiteness reveals the true spiritual nature of sin.

The Conquest of Sin

When we say that we do not derive biological death from an original fault, this is not to deny the reality of sin. This original fault or even our personal sins in no way concerns our mortal nature. The agony of sin (distinguished here from the agony of death) or the temptation to despair is enclosed in this non sinful mortality. "To die the death" of *Genesis 2:17* is not simply to die but to suffer death to the point of dying because of it. If this is so, then many theological interpretations go by the board. That of the consequence of sin is less biological death than the suffering of separation experienced in death. The agony of death is not uniquely to die physically but not to know how to live one's death without being totally enclosed within it. We must know how to live our death without being enclosed totally within it. Not to be able to do this causes the agony of death.

To the "better to die than to sin" as the true meaning of the divine sentence is not a question of substituting a "we die because we have sinned" at the risk of understanding nothing of sin or death in *Genesis*. Engrafted on biological death, the agony of sin takes a position, as an army conquering a territory which has been neutral. The acceptance or offering one's death to another (his Father) rather than the refusal or rebellion against nonsense: such is the crucial alternative which Christ makes on his way from Gethsemene to Golgotha. A death freely given not in rebellion but not totally enclosed with death: "Father, into thy hands."

21

It is in light of these reflections that we must see the agony of Jesus in the Garden of Olives. First, Jesus does not resign himself to death as a lamb to be immolated to satisfy the anger of a vengeful Father. He fully gives his life by taking upon himself the refusal of men before their God, refusal of their creatureliness and limitations. Jesus moreover does not confront the cross as a sublime test in the certitude of his resurrection. He abandons himself in full confidence to his Father by fidelity to the filial relationship and not by the knowledge of a scenario which he already knows will come to pass. Finally, Jesus does not perfect his life by an act of death as the ultimate signature of a work which would perdure through the memory of men. The meaning of his life given and totally offered would then disappear behind the triumphal heroism of him who, making believe that he gave his life, takes it back immediately to confer on it a meaning which he himself and only he has willed. In reality and truth, Christ simply abandons himself in trust to the Father who is the God of the living and not of the dead. That's it and that's all of it.

The evangelical text resists all these interpretations and imposes a silence upon us before the agony which being unique by the person of the Son confronts it for us all, is nonetheless profoundly human. Neither resigned to his disappearance nor certain of his resurrection, nor heroic in its perfection, Christ suffers in reality the agony of death which everyone suffers in the felt imminence of his own end: "Arriving at the place called Gethsemene, he said to his disciples, 'stay here while I pray'. And taking with him Peter, James and John, he began to be full of fear and agony" (*Mark 14:32-33*).

Fear in Greek (*thambos*) has a triple meaning for him who experiences it by making him recede before the menace which is coming (assassination, accident, sickness, condemned to death);

then to abandon oneself to the sentiment of precariousness of his own existence (as one condemned to death no longer knowing why he must live in the face of the unique sentence of death); finally a desire to share with others one's fear.

In such meanings and for each one Christ probably was afraid at the threshold of his own death. Thus it was necessary for him to recoil before the menace of the "cup" that he knew he had to drink to the last: "Abba, Father, all things are possible for you, take this cup from me" (*Mark 14:36*). The second trait of fear - abandoning himself to the sadness of a life which can never be consoled, which can be perfected only in death: "My soul is sad even unto death" (*14:34*). But also he seeks to share his fear - third trait - but there is no one, neither disciples nor apostles, who respond to his urgent appeal when everything is absent from him. He comes to his disciples three times and three times he begs them with the same invocation: "Simon, are you asleep" (*14:37,40,41*). At the last, suddenly, the victory is acquired: "Sleep now and rest. It is done." What is this "it is done"? So that Jesus can tell them to rest? If not, the sorrowful passage to the awful agony (*ademonia*) which he experiences alone but in an uninterrupted dialogue with his Father.

The Anguished Christ

"Taking with him Peter, James and John, he began to be overcome with fear and agony." Here agony does not have a triple particularity - contrary to the traits of fear - but leaves the person confronted with an indeterminate object of his agony (as one who sobs does not know why he is crying); agony reveals to him the void, the nothingness of his existence; and finally agony is to isolate him altogether from the ensemble of humans whom he must leave.

Christ was in agony not only in regard to the imminence of his death but, more, in the retrospective vision of his own life. Thus he had to renounce the reasons for his fear. He had to go

23

from "if it be possible that this cup pass from me," the Son had to go in intimate dialogue with his Father, to "if it is not possible that it pass from me without my drinking it" (*Matthew 26:39,42*). Then the Son submits, abandons himself freely, goes from fear to agony, there where that of which he is afraid becomes totally indeterminate. "Not as I will but as you will." (*Mark 14:36*).

Thus he is plunged into the emptiness of his *kenosis*: "But he emptied himself taking the form of a salve" (*Philippians 2:7*) depriving himself of his glory that he had with the Father from the beginning so that he could become man. "All is finished" as the last words of Christ on the cross (*John 19:30*) thus designates that "I am ended living" by which the Son gives himself completely to the Father for entering fully but deliberately into the abasement of his *kenosis*. Christ here reaches the nadir of *kenosis* in the mystery of the incarnation.

But contrary to fear or agony, isolated in that agony is not such that he breaks his relationship with his Father. It is precisely in his absolute aloneness where lies the paroxysm of his communion. *Kenosis,* freely given, trust in his Father in the midst of agony.

Abandon and Communion

In the midst of the multiple appeals of Christ to his God, the Father in effect does not cease remaining Father for his Son. First in the cry uttered toward his God: "My God, My God, why have you abandoned me?" (*Mark 15:34*) followed by "Abba, Father" that the Son implores that the cup be taken from him (Abba = the proper father of him who speaks), finally in the last words of Christ on the cross, "Father, into thy hands I commend my spirit" (*Luke 23:46*). At Gethsemene as on Golgotha, God teaches himself as man. It is not the Son who loses his Father as if he doubted God but it is man separated from God that Jesus experiences in his humanity going to man.

Thus the death of Jesus is not only "his" in the sense that it belongs to him alone (as to every man, to die to die to be born). It also reveals his being tot he world when he gives and freely offers in a sinless manner, this very life in which is enclosed every man in imminence of the end: "No one takes my life because it is I who give it" (*John 10:18*). The self gift of Christ designates only but fully the modality which is at the same time the most ordinary and the most exemplary of his proper existence. No one takes Christ's life because he gives it freely such that the ultimate reversal designates the act by which, deliberately, he gives himself to finitude which he freely accepts and to his Father. By giving his being as gift to the point of abandonment to the Father. In trust and confidence Christ abandons himself to his Father: "Father, into thy hands I commend my spirit."

CHAPTER VI
THE GOD WHO SUFFERS

Of all the arguments given against the existence of a personal and loving God, suffering is the most powerful because it is emotional. Emotions go to the heart and the heart gives us the truth about who we are.

If we remain at the rational-intellectual level, we never go beyond the surface, the superficial as explanation. Because in the final analysis, there is no rational explanation of suffering. As Dostoevsky said, the world is not worth the suffering of even one child.

There are all forms of suffering: mental suffering, physical suffering, loneliness, spiritual emptiness, boredom, feelings of futility and failure/loss, love lost and never found, emptiness for what we do not know. There is always the spiritual emptiness of the soul that seeks fulfillment in material things, power, wealth, diversions, sex, good times, fine food, etc. but is never satiated, never satisfied. It is principally from this suffering that we feel wounded and grieving which nothing seems able to fill or satisfy. The suffering of a child brings this to the fore most poignantly because we know what he/she does not know: there is no answer to his suffering which has escaped the minds of the most brilliant of our race. It has become such a stumbling block, that many have opted either for the *nothingness* and futility of human freedom (atheism) or have sought to overcome desire/suffering by surrender to the oneness of all things in compassion and peace (Buddhism).

When it comes to suffering, the monotheists (Judaism, Islam, Christianity) have the most formidable task of reconciling the reality of suffering with a personal, compassionate, loving God who is unconditional in his love as revealed by the central religious figures of Moses, Christ and Mohammed. I speak here of the Christian response to this reality of suffering in our lives.

Clearly, the very act of our creation made in the image and likeness of God creates in us a dimension that can be satisfied only in reference to whom and in whose image we have been created. That flows from the very nature of our creation and is, in that sense, the foundation and reason for all human suffering which I shall try to explain. Until we are united to the one in whose image we have been created, that spiritual emptiness occupies our souls night and day, each hour of every day. We try and fill that spiritual emptiness with that which cannot satisfy: material things, sex, power, wealth, even spouses, family, children. All individually or taken together cannot fill the void of our being. "You have made our hearts for yourself and they are restless until they rest in you" as Saint Augustine put it.

The Christian religion holds what Jesus has revealed to us about God: the unspeakable, unutterable mystery who is our origin, created others to love him freely and intelligently because he is love. This mystery has created not out of necessity but freely (there can be no love without freedom) in function of who and what he is: love. In other words, love is not a characteristic of God but is his very being, his essence, his reality which we cannot fathom or measure. Jesus has revealed to us that this unutterable mystery is benevolent Father, Abba, whose love is unconditional because that is his nature. There is not a time when God does not love us from all eternity and there will be not be a time when God shall have refused to love us. The prodigal son in the gospel has only to turn and *recognize* what was there from the beginning: the father's unconditional love and forgiveness. It is impossible that that love one day was and another day was not.

The revelation of Jesus consists simply in this: God is Father, Abba, who loves absolutely and unconditionally. Forgiveness always at the ready precisely because of who God is. He *is* love not just one who has love for us. Love is not a characteristic of God as is his creativeness, his knowledge, his power; he is love as his very substance so that forgiveness is the other side of the

27

reality of love. The gospels constantly come back to that theme: God at the ready to receive the prodigal son because God already loved without condition. The son had only to turn to recognize what was always there, never absent.

Thus the creative act of God made man out of and for love. God creates to share his love which must be, like that of God, on the part of man, an absolutely free response. Love can be nothing other than free. God suffers therefore in an analogical sense because his creative love is never fully requited by the created creator. The rejection of this love causes God to suffer as does his own inability to force his love on man who is free to return that love or not. God risks in creating man. He risked the nature of his very creation who was created free to accept or reject him. This risk is suffering that the love often has not been returned.

Therefore from all eternity God has willed his Son to become one of us to show us concretely that face of love and forgiveness and to share the suffering from man's violence and unrequited love.

What is man's violence but not only the refusal to love God but the willingness to destroy whom we should love made in God's image. That image is destroyed and perverted by man's violence who seeks to destroy what was created to be loved. In that very real but analogical sense, God suffers in his love and in and through the suffering Christ who accepts freely and lovingly all the violence of men into his being without rancor or vengeance or hate; but in forgiveness and reconciliation.

Jesus has come not to explain suffering or to take it away but to endure it with us because we do not love enough or even (God forbid!) not at all. That is the real core of human suffering because it reflects who we are as images of God. The suffering God in the face of the suffering Christ who is with suffering humanity until the end of time.

Jesus as the Incarnate, suffering Word is the great scandal of the world. How could God be crucified and humiliated on an infamous gibbet? This is mockery for intellectuals, a stumbling block for Jews and Muslims. As far back as the second century the great Roman intellectual Celsus held that it was impossible for God to feel such pain and suffering. He dismissed as simply absurd the whole notion that the inimitable and ineffable God who created the universe could somehow be born, cry, bleed and die ignominiously. Yet God did not disdain participation in our sad realities, solidarity with our death, companion of our suffering, going down to hell, that is, to the pure hopelessness and domination of violence and death, who gave all in love for his spouse who is the human race. It is God who feels to its dregs all the crucifixion of human existence in flesh and blood *to make it God's own*. There is no way to rationally understand any of this. None of us can. But God did it to be one with us to the very core of our death so he can raise it to glory with him, for us. If none of this is true, then Christians are the most miserable of all men, of all religions. Christianity stands or falls on the very notion of our human absurdity: a suffering God.

That is the key to understanding suffering. That is why the Church can cry in the darkest moment of the liturgy while Christ is liturgically still in the clutches of death, "Oh happy fault of Adam that has merited for us such a Savior."

CHAPTER VII
THE LAW OF THE CROSS

The cost of discipleship in *Luke 14:25-33* is so demanding that we must prefer Christ even to our own lives, even to that of our closest relatives. If necessary, we must be prepared to prefer Christ even to our own family. Clearly Christ is not asking us to abandon those we love dearest - we are bound by ties of kinship and justice which make firm demands upon us. Even Christ warned of false piety that would abandon the Fifth Commandment of honoring parents in order to observe some religious law about dedication of money to the temple. Nonsense, says Christ, we cannot so abrogate the commandments of God. To love father and mother is a divine command.

But there could come a time that to save ourselves or even our families, we would have to deny Christ. That is the preference Christ is talking about. It is difficult to think of such a situation actually coming about, but Christ emphasizes that if it does, we must prefer his confession above all other values - even our own lives or those of our loved ones. That's a terrible demand so Christ tells his disciples, think about that carefully before you become my disciple. Calculate like a general with 10,000 men, if he can meet a force of 20,000. If you can't, *don't commit*. It is perhaps the only place in the Gospel where Christ warns *against* becoming one of his disciples because of the price of discipleship. Either go all the way or don't commit. Don't start building an edifice you can't complete. That's foolish and stupid. It is one thing to be laughed at because of the foolishness of the cross; it is another because we didn't have the gumption to complete what we started.

Christ says that to be his disciple - and that decision has to be made by each disciple personally - the price is very heavy. Most never even think about it. They were born and brought up Catholic - so what? They go to church, give a little, receive the sacraments. No big deal. That all costs little. They never encounter a situation in life where discipleship costs them dearly and so they never make a real decision for or against Christ in their whole lives. That is what Bonhoefer called "cheap grace" which is no discipleship at all. That is because there has been no learning or accepting the law of the cross. "I'm a good Catholic" amounts to nothing more than some rituals and practices that free us from the responsibility of acting like Christ.

Jesus goes to Jerusalem. He knows what awaits him at the end of the road and knows the situation very well: his cross means that love must subject itself to violence rather than respond to it in kind with a new violence. Love will put violence to death by ending it here and now, by not responding to it in kind, by ending it in Christ. By not passing it on, violence dies in me. That is a terrible decision because it goes against everything in my being, everything in nature to respond to violence with violence. That is not the way of the cross. The ultimate truth of man is love and there is no love unless one gives self totally. Love is total gift or it is nothing but sentimentality or sensuality of the moment. When you give yourself totally, there is nothing to take back.

Thus the language of the cross is very difficult to understand let alone put into practice. It is sovereign force but it takes the accents of the greatest weakness. It is complete power expressed in abject humiliation and powerlessness. *The cross contradicts all our human instincts, even the best.* The spirit of competition, our desire to be first, to dominate others, to prefer ourselves over all others, our cult to have and to appear great among others and in the eyes of others. The cross contradicts these deepest of human instincts and that is why we attempt to cover or substitute this law of the cross with religion, rituals and rotes. Not that these are bad - they are good but only after we have accepted the terrible law of the cross in our lives.

Christ proposes this law of the cross to us but he knew that in proposing such a demand, he instigates the murderous refusal of those who do not desire such a peace and those who even among

31

Christians have made a compromise with the world. The cross is at the same time an expose of violence and the demonstration of its perversity: Christ accepts the lot laid out for him by the forces of evil. He has become intolerable for them because they are violent. The violent man cannot accomplish the justice of God because that is to impose his will on others. God never acts violently - it is against his very nature of love. God can only act lovingly, patiently, mercifully and justfully, because he is love. To act violently is to act unlike God. So Christ on the cross accepts the unjust violence of evil men and returns it not, thereby forever destroying violence in his very person.

Thus how true the statement of Paul: who can accept such foolishness, such stupidity that goes forthrightly against the wisdom of the world: prefer yourself, protect yourself, conserve yourself and yours? Christ says, lose yourselves and you will be saved: "Who loses his soul for my sake shall find it and who finds his soul shall lose it."

Therefore there will always be conflict and division over Christ and the way of the cross - and over Christians who choose to follow "the way." This is particularly true when this law of the cross confronts the ways of religion and piety which substitutes religion and ritual for the law of the cross. That is extremely easy to do because it is a natural thing to do. To escape the terrible demands of the cross we substitute ritual and religion. This will even produce division in families, in communities and above all, in ourselves *because there is in each one of us something that wants to impose ourselves on others*, dominate others, subject others to our will. All of us want to be God. But that is not how God acts.

That is why we must prefer Christ's way rather than our own way, even to our own lives. Paradoxically, we love others better, purer, completely, in preferring Christ over all the rest. To prefer Christ over our own lives is *to love life beyond its very limits*. This Christ is not in competition

32

with ourselves nor with those we love. That is absurd. In preferring Christ, we prefer what is best and holy for those we love because in following Christ alone is peace and joy and fulfillment. There are ways of loving which are contrary to love because such ways depend on us ourselves and on the satisfaction that we draw from others and not on the way Christ loves us and them.

Jesus is well aware of the great difficulties in his demand to follow him, the price of true discipleship which we have described. Christ is under no illusion that "many are called but few are chosen." All are called to be Christ's disciples but before doing so, each should consider the very heavy price that must be paid. No cheap grace here. If the real truth of the Gospel were known with its demands, would there be that many Christians? It is a legitimate question but one that cannot be answered.

We may have full commitment to Christ but there will always be falls, difficult times and delays. None of us are perfect while we are on the way. Why else do we see first in entering any Catholic church, a confessional? Or why is it that the most sacred rituals-symbol of Catholicism, the Mass, begins with an admission that we are sinners and must confess that to each other? Even during the passion, the disciples fled. Only later did they learn completely; their hour would come later. To the patience of God must be added our own patience - with ourselves.

SECTION II

THE RESURRECTION OF JESUS

CHAPTER VIII
THE TRANSFIGURATION

Paul tells us that God's purpose and design for humanity was always good news, positive and joyful, that God has made man for himself and has continuously led humanity in history to himself whose journey would culminate in the visibility of this salvific purpose in Christ Jesus, the Incarnate Word of God (*II Timothy 1:8-10*). Everything is orientated to Jesus; all human history receives its culmination and meaning in Jesus. This grace of God has now become visible to our eyes in Jesus. This revelation has known its last word by the destruction of death, making life resplendent in immortality. All human history has but one tenet, one goal and that is the emergence of Christ in Jesus of Nazareth, the pascal work - which is the announcement and the heart of the good news. Clearly, the story of Abraham leaving his country by the call of God on the faith of a promise is part of this long story of the design of God. But Jesus marks the decisive stage of this secret from all ages revealed now, visibly, in Christ Jesus. This mystery constituted an elect people who waited for Christ. As Jesus told the disciples as they walked to Emmaus the evening of the first Easter, that the law and all the Scriptures spoke of him. He was in a sense already there. "Before Abraham came to be, I am" (*John 8:58*).

In *Matthew 17:1-9* we have the story of the Transfiguration, visible to human eyes where the light becomes blinding. In fact it was the Transfiguration which was the splendor which Jesus had at every moment as Incarnate Word, hidden in flesh and now revealed for a moment. His face was hidden in earthly life but here it was allowed to shine in all its radiance. The power of the work of the resurrection to come enlightens the whole Gospel. Even at Christ's birth we can see this: "For today in the city of David there has been born for you a Savior who is Christ the Lord" (*Luke 2:11*). How could the child be "Lord" (resurrection) except that the whole Gospel is now read or re-read in light of the resurrection itself? The Christ Child is already 'Lord' since all the events including the resurrection has already happened and Luke re-reads in light of that event.. The disciples when they left all things to follow Christ, already suspected this without fully being able to articulate it. The Transfiguration anticipates this without fully being able to articulate it. The Transfiguration anticipates the glory of the resurrection and renders it visible. The resurrection was not as explicit as the Transfiguration: the glory of the resurrection remains hidden. The astonishing formula of *II Peter 1:14* to authenticate his message, relies not on the resurrection which one would expect but on the transfiguration which gives the meaning of the resurrection. Thus the last word of this chapter: the disciples must say nothing of the vision before the Son of man is raised from the dead. The Transfiguration is an anticipation of the glory of the resurrection which will be understood only after the crucifixion and death of Jesus. They must wait till then to reveal it.

The law and the prophets are there, all that preceded Jesus. Peter, James and John are also there. All history is recapitulated here. But Peter wants to stop there, he wants to stop history and build tabernacles where the glory of Jesus was manifested. The cloud covering the scene is that of *Exodus* which in contrary to stopping. Exodus was an essential *going forward* to the Promised Land.

Peter must descend from the mountain, re-find Jesus and walk together toward Jerusalem which waits for Christ in order to crucify him. Jerusalem where Peter does not want to go for what Christ promised would be there. Not glory but ignominious death at the hands of the Jewish priests and foreigners. This was a total shock to Peter after he had just witnessed the glory of Jesus in the Transfiguration. How could this Be? Peter rejects what awaits Jesus there because it destroyed his view of the Messiah who would come in glory to destroy Israel's enemies (*Matthew 16:21-23*). That is why Christ rejects the worldly thought of glory of Peter who seeks to avoid the mission of Jesus who is to go to Jerusalem and be crucified: "Far be it for you to do such a thing" is the rebuke of Peter. Christ calls Peter's desire a desire of the devil who seeks to deter Christ from his terrible mission of the cross. The voice from heaven confirms the mission of Jesus, "hear him." This voice designates Jesus as the one whom we must follow, the Christ of the resurrection. But he is also the Christ of the cross which we must take up daily and follow him to Calvary. There is no other way to the resurrection except through the cross. Only then can we with Christ participate in his resurrection. That is why the Church preaches Christ, and him crucified. No other way to follow Christ.

Transfiguration = Cross = Resurrection!

CHAPTER IX
REFLECTIONS ON THE PASSION, DEATH AND RESURRECTION OF JESUS

All three synoptic Gospels tell of the last supper as a pascal meal, the ritualistic commemoration of the meal taken by the Israelites on the night before they were to leave Egypt. Just as the Israelites escaped slavery by means of crossing the desert which was really a crossing over of death, so too Christ, bearer in himself of a whole new people, is going to accomplish an exodus, a crossing over from death. But why the blood of a lamb? Perhaps to emphasize the profound meaning of exodus: true liberation is the liberation from death. Each year the Jews were to commemorate, memorialize this event by the rite of the lamb. Jesus will put an end to this ritual because his own flesh and blood would replace that of the lamb. But this flesh and blood of Jesus is accessible only through vegetative nourishment: bread and wine. By subjecting himself to violence, Jesus overcomes violence.

Everything was in place for the murder: the jealousy of the leaders of the nation (*Matthew 27:18)*; the greed of Judas; the laxity of the disciples; the nothingness of Herod; the political opportunism of Pilate, the fickleness of the people. The putting to death of Jesus is inscribed in the events and in the hearts of men. Politics and religion join together for their evil deed. Jesus finds himself in an impasse: he can escape but he chooses not to. Death having become inevitable, Jesus chooses it freely, voluntarily. That is why the last supper precedes the whole chain of events which will lead to the crucifixion. Judas delivers Christ to the high priests; the high priests deliver him to Pilate; Pilate delivers him to the mob demanding his crucifixion. But before all the others, Jesus freely delivers himself: "take and eat, this is my flesh, this is my blood." "No one takes my life except I give it freely" (*John 10:18)*. Men *think* that they are taking the life of Jesus whereas in reality they will receive it as a gift, as nourishment for their lives.

In light of this free decision of Christ, we learn that the Almighty God submits himself to the decision of men. He makes himself prey to our freedom. He lets himself be killed, eliminated form our lives, from our villages, from our homes. God is with us to the very end and makes his own all our ways without issue because he himself is the issue. Letting himself be crushed by the violence of men instead of responding in kind by violence, force and power, God breaks the infernal cycle of violence which engenders more violence. By not responding, by absorbing the violence into himself he destroys it. In this way, love becomes manifest. At the last supper we see this love which is none other than God delivering himself who is true nourishment of man, that is, what makes man live and maintains him in life. When we take the bread and wine in memory of Christ, that means that we make our own the law of love. Participate in the Eucharist is to receive a gift and to commit ourselves to cultivate in us those attitudes which were in Christ Jesus. Instead of the food becoming us like ordinary food; we commit ourselves to become the food, Christ with his attitudes and convictions: "I live now not I but Christ lives in me."

The Jesus is affixed to a tree above the earth to be seen in humiliation by jokers and scoffers. Those who passed hardly even noticed - or cared because it was none of their business. But it is our affair! We have killed him in others by despising them or abandoning them in their distress. The cross is the work of men, not of God. Of all men for what is truly universal and by which we resemble one another of whatever religion we are, is our cruelty or indifference to each other, toward the brothers. Jews (high priests) and pagans (Pilate) are in agreement to crucify the just one. Act of man but also act of God. It is the divine act by which Absolute love without measure is revealed.

God whom we call Father does not wish the death of his Son but generates him eternally in life. God does not seek vengeance nor satisfaction of any sense of justice by shedding his blood.

He has refused the blood of animals by the prophets, how much more would he refuse human blood? He desires no ransom (the death of his Son) so that his other sons can be relieved of their debt to him. These images are just that, images of biblical metaphors which must be left behind. The truth of God to which Christ bears witness to on the cross, is the truth of love: no longer the law of talion which demands equivalence between the sin and its compensation, but absolute grace. The cross is God who gratuitously by grace comes to espouse the destiny of all those that human frailty has caused to suffer, to all those whom we have dehumanized by dehumanizing ourselves. Victims of our desire to dominate, to refuse others a share in the goods we possess. God who strips himself of glory comes to be affixed on a cross as figure of all victims.

Love demands of him who loves that he share the lot of the beloved. God has always been God with us. On the cross he manifests that he has gone with us "all the way" to the extreme limit of our weakness. Henceforth no man no matter what his pain or distress can ever say that he is alone. No matter the hell to which we have descended, we will find Christ there who has preceded us there and awaits us. This dispossession of Christ is not some sort of accident. This dispossession says something about God himself: gift of life, gift of self so that the other - we - can live from his given life. The marvel is that this given life, this life that God loses in giving it, this life in whose image we must give, is not lost but saved. God being love becomes more God in giving himself, so to speak. Grace more abounds. Love more abounds. Christ is never more Christ that when he says 'this is my flesh given up for you; this is my blood poured out for you.' This is exactly what happened on the cross and finds there its significance.

Life is stronger than death. The texts on the resurrection are calm - after the turmoil of Good Friday. After the night which represents the power of darkness, we are early in the morning at first light. "The first day of the week" refers us back to *Genesis* when God illuminates by creating the first day. In *Genesis* the light arises from nothing whereas in the Gospels Christ-light arises from the tomb which is also darkness but which signifies that there has been a death, that there was a murder, destruction of the work of God. The creative Word of *Genesis,* the Word who is Christ himself, was denied. But the Word of God cannot be chained even by death. Therefore a new morning, a new dawn of time. A new man.

We must repeat it often that the resurrection is the core of our faith. Every day we have death before our eyes as the horizon of everything we do or say. Death speaks. It tells us that we live in vain, that the last word is our destruction from the face of the earth. This appearance of death is given the lie by Christian faith because God does not create in view of death. Life and death are incompatible because God is life. Center of our faith, the resurrection is also a stumbling block. We know what we are saying when we say 'death' but we do not know what we are saying when we say resurrection. It is a simple affirmation: "This Jesus who was dead is alive." How does he live? We have no response because we cannot understand what life in God is. If resurrection establishes our faith it is also the foundation of our hope and in that there is total joy which can co-habit with our worst distress and pain.

The scriptural signs of the resurrection are significant. Our Gospel as yet does not speak of apparitions. We are at the tomb which is open and empty with the mortuary linens. The empty tomb tells us that Jesus is not to be looked for among the dead. 'Why do you seek among the dead he who is living?" (*Luke 24:5*). This earthly place also says absolution of God for the murder: the body of the crime (the *corpus delicti*) has disappeared. Amnesty but also annulment of the process which condemned Christ. That is why the linens were folded in their place as if nothing had happened, as if no one had laid there. Simply this memorial is inseparable from the memory of pardon. The stone which closed the tomb has been rolled back: the tomb as image of darkness and death, communicates with the external world, that of life, of light, of open tomb. The open tomb is the image of liberation. It turns us back to the exodus from Egypt.

> "...he himself likewise also partook of the same, that through death he might render powerless him who had the power of death, that is, the devil; and might deliver those who through fear of death were subject to slavery all their lives" (*Hebrews 2:14-15*).

In and by the resurrection we are free, free of the fear of death and now a future open to absolute life.

Mystery because it is God's life but reality which is foundation of our hope.

CHAPTER X
THE PASCAL MYSTERY

Of all the religions of the world, Christianity is founded on one who was ignominiously put to death as a criminal on a Roman cross. The first disciples and founders of that religion were all cowards who ran at the first sight of men's violence and power against their master.

Think about that for a moment. Most religions love to adulate and magnify their founders, how perfect were the founder's disciples, how glorious and miraculous the outcome. Just the opposite in the Christian religion. And were it not true, the recorders of the events of the life and death of Jesus Christ would never have narrated it. No one narrates humiliation, defeat, cowardice, fear, abandonment and death as foundation of religion. Who would believe or accept it? One believes something because it is true and no one would believe it were it not true. The very first disciple, on whom Christ would build his church, was a coward, a public betrayer not once but three times. Were it not for the fact that it was Christ who forgave him and reinstated him, no one would have accepted his authority in Christ's community.

The second marvelous point (which so many Christians have neglected or simply rejected) is that the proof of faith in Christ is love/service of the brothers and the sisters. Christ came not to glorify himself, not to receive adulation and praise but to serve and to give an example to all his disciples that their way must not be the way of power, domination, might and glory of temporal rulers; but service as a slave-servant after the very example of Jesus who came to give his life as a ransom for many. He comes into Jerusalem not in triumph but on the foal of a jackass; he forbids those on whom he confers healing to announce that he is Messiah because others would misunderstand; he washes the feet of his disciples to give them an example of service and of love;

he gives everything he has including his life on a humiliating Roman gibbet between two malefactors as sign of his love for all. We too, he tells us, must be prepared to lay down our lives for our brothers whether that is actually martyrdom in blood as witness to faith or bloodless martyrdom of lifelong service for our fellow men: "By this shall all men know that you are my disciples, that you love one another." That love can be, must be, proven by a loving and giving service or the faith is shown to be false and superficial.

The third momentous aspect of the high holy days is that Christ gives himself over, freely, willingly to the violence and hatred of men who murder him. He responds only in love and forgiveness, not hatred and vengeance - and therein is the glory of the redemptive act. A philosopher once said - and I agree fully with him - that he could never believe in a father who would kill or sacrifice his own son to satisfy his own vengeance. That perverted theology has gotten Christianity a lot of bad press and needless scandal. We are saved by the love of Christ for us which is also the love of the Father, who fully gives himself over to the violence and hatred of men, to take it all upon himself and to die from it and by his resurrection, to put it forever to death. Because he loved, Jesus gave all he had including his life and refused not only to pass on that hatred but absorbed it into his very being, taking it down to hell in his death and to rise triumphant over death and hatred. Christians are to do like Christ: love, give, serve, forgive, absorb hatred and vengeance and to die to all these so that they too in and with Christ, may put to death, death/sin in their own lives. Only then can they rise with him.

That is the meaning of redemption - not some bloody vengeful demand by a spiteful God for equalizing justice and payment for sin, a form of blood lust. Unless redemption is seen in the light of the unutterable love of the Father in Christ Jesus, we distort the whole redemptive act: "God so loves the world that he gave his only begotten Son" (*John 3:16*). Gave him to what? Gave him over to the free hatred and violence of men so that absorbing it in his very person, he may forever put it to death for all those who believe in him, i.e. those who love following the very example and practice of Jesus. They will also rise with him.

That is the meaning of these three sacred days which sum up the pascal mystery for Christians. Holy Thursday as the example of servanthood, for love of the brothers; Good Friday as total and free gift even to the hatred and violence of men, dying in agony but with total trust and obedience to the Father. Easter as God's 'yes' to his Christ and to us in the resurrection from death, having put death to death, the death that comes from hatred and violence. In the midst of the darkest days, the cry is heard, "Victory is ours." That is why it is "Good" Friday.

One may of course reject all this a the perfect myth, the projection of our deepest desires and hopes and dreams, but myth nonetheless. Denial or acceptance, it is always a matter of faith. A faith that reaches to the depths of our profoundest hopes.

Personally, I am always tempted not to believe, not because it is hard to believe - it is always hard to believe for we are made to know not to believe; we believe because we must, because we reach beyond all that is human to the mystery of God himself and only God can speak to us of God. I am tempted to un-belief because the pascal mystery is too good to be true. Like the disciples when they saw the resurrected Lord, "their joy was so great that they could not believe it" (*Luke 24:41*).

The un-believer may die from the agony of un-belief; the believer dies from the utter joy of belief. Either way, we must die and we choose the way we die. One is the despair of the absurd and the night; the other is the confidence and trust in the God of life and love.

CHAPTER XI
PASCAL GLADNESS, PASCAL PROCLAMATION

Christ is risen. It was a cry, a murmur, a rumor, a breaking forth, a proclamation. It is news that burns in the heart and spreads like a forest fire from generation to generation even up to today.

Tombs are places destined to maintain the remembrance of the dead. What would the tomb of Jesus be if the faith of the Christian communities for twenty centuries had not proclaimed him living, beyond death? Living not only in our hearts by the remembrance of those who think that his message merits to be heard yet, but living also in that humanity which made him part of us even to our very flesh. I ask myself: if I didn't think of Christ living in this latter sense, why visit the tomb in Jerusalem? Why bother at all except perhaps for historical curiosity? It would lead me, well, to despair.

The four Gospels speak of this tomb of Jesus. Carved from a rock says Mark. Belonging to Joseph of Arimethea - that secret disciple of Jesus who came out at the end. A new tomb says Matthew and John. John insists on this: no body had laid in it. New because it was necessary to understand the message of the words of Jesus which during his earthly abode were not understood; "Behold I make all things new" (*Revelations 21:5*). It is the new creation begun in this unique event.

I should have liked to see the garden during the spring where Mary Magdalen wandered that morning of the first day of the week. It was dawn notes the Gospel of John. In her heart there was yet the night of a grief which would not stop because the one who disappeared had taken with him an unheard of hope. Of him, we hear nothing more; we do not even have the trace of his body on which is read for better or for worse, the traits of the beloved while he was yet alive. The garden was full of flowers that spring morning. The gardener walked about. His question was not strange under the circumstances: "Who are you looking for?" The voice is strange yet the same voice with an entirely different accent and then it becomes an appeal as unexpected as can be: "Mary." It is the accent of him who always called his disciples by their name, the name which speaks of their singularity and incomparable value in his eyes and of every human being. This was a personal, face to face, indivisible encounter between the two.

Everything then begins. It is truly the first morning of the world, of the new world, the new creation. In the symbol of *Genesis*, there too was a garden at the dawn of humanity where Yahweh walked. Did Mary Magdalen understand this? It was not a return to life as before and that is why it does not serve any purpose to seek to hold on to Jesus whose voice resembles so perfectly that of the rabbi who was so human, so close during those three years. It is a new creation. Paul proclaimed it later: "The old world has passed away, a new reality is here" (*II Corinthians 5:17*).

The recitals of the resurrection, that is, the manifestations of the resurrected one, occupy very little space in the Gospels compared to the chapter on the proceedings and the passion of Jesus: two chapters in Matthew, two in Mark, two in Luke and two in John. If the resurrected one had simply reappeared on the scene of history, if he had taken revenge on his adversaries, if he had returned the crowds to his favor and walked in triumph into the streets of Jerusalem- what an historical event that would have been! What newsprint to roll! If there had been cameras and TV, what first stories in screens around the whole world! That was not possible.

Theologians speak in their jargon of a "trans-historical event." In other words, the resurrection is beyond history but which has infiltrated into our history. Because it was beyond history it could only arise among us as a blink of an eye.

It is enough for us to say that this new humanity is henceforth our own, hidden as a tree in an acorn, infinitely discrete as the flower in the bulb. Of this newness that surpassed all representation, we are the witnesses. And it is very true that without this newness which is impossible for me to represent exactly, I would be forced to say that Christianity is nothing more than a system of thought and action just like all the rest. And as futile to ultimate meaning. This is what Paul meant when he offered that proclamation come down through all the ages: "If Christ is not risen, our preaching is vain and empty is your faith" (*I Corinthians 15:14*). That says it all in one short sentence. Outside of it, there is only another set of wisdom literature, a wisdom but not an adherence which is called *faith*.

Eternal life has already begun, says one of the liturgical texts. In the final analysis, this is the only thing that interests me even if I have great sympathy for those who in their own way, are interested in "the Jesus of history" as an unequaled model but only a model of humanity. What excites me, passions me, is the testimony of those who have seen and touched him under the traits of a humanity banally human and earthly, simple, apparently too simple, too close to our human existence: a gardener at the dawn of a spring day; a pilgrim on the road when two men walk to Emmaus and in whom all hope had been crushed where night came to efface everything they had lived for; an unknown person along the shore of the Lake of Galilee in the early morning with a meal prepared for his friends with a morsel of bread and a piece of broiled fish. All too human but in whom they recognized, "it is the Lord."

Where is he, this Christ whom the resurrection rendered totally other here on earth, where men and women pine and rejoice, cry over ruins and yet work for the future? The event of the end of time is already begun, already accomplished. Our history continues. The resurrected one is outside of our history which we await even while we live and work for one another..

Before that empty tomb it was said to the women what the disciples took to be an

48

hallucination: "He precedes you in Galilee." Beautiful and rustic Galilee. A Galilee that we now know was not only a cross roads where pagans and Jews crossed but a place of resistance to the Romans. Jesus heard the groans of revolt of the little people against the occupiers and their accomplices. A Galilee where Jesus knew the lake with its calmness and sudden tempests, the lilies of the valley and their beautiful allure. A Galilee where Jesus lived with the company of artists and artisans. A Galilee where he learned the life of a man, of a profession, of a Jew before he becomes an itinerant rabbi and preacher of the Kingdom of God. A Galilee from which he drew all his materials for his incomparable parables through which we are presented with a kingdom made for man, taking for that purpose the most humble experiences of life of ordinary men and women of our earth.

In this way I can believe in a resurrected one who is and remains forever *the* Galilean. And I know like every man from every place and from all time, that I can accept that Jesus sowed eternity into the earth and its history, where my human roots are and always will be. He eternalized that earth and that history.

I worship and weep in silence. Amen.

CHAPTER XII
PETER'S WITNESS OF THE RESURRECTION

After the events of the passion and a great silence that follows, Peter according to Mark, reappears and in a certain way, he is the privileged witness of the resurrection. In fact, the message given by the two angels in white to the women who come to anoint Jesus and who discovered the tomb empty, Peter is the only disciple mentioned by name: "Why do you seek the living among the dead? He is not here...Go tell his disciples and Peter and he (Jesus) precedes you into Galilee; there you will see him as he told you."

All seems to be forgotten about Peter's betrayal during the passion as if the mention of Peter by the messengers not only re-integrates Peter into the group of his disciples, but also integrates him into the new relationship that he will henceforth have with Jesus.

In different circumstances, Luke confirms this. In this encounter with the resurrected one (*Luke 24: 13-35*), the disciples from Emmaus are heard to say to the eleven and those who were with them that "the Lord is truly risen (from the dead) and was seen by Simon" (*Luke 24: 33-34*). This priority of apparition given to Peter is in its turn confirmed by Paul at the end of his first epistle to the Corinthians in a formula which is particularly significant because it is a confession of faith. Paul proclaims "Christ died for our sins according to the Scriptures and he was buried and he rose on the third day according to the Scriptures and that he appeared to Cephas, then to the twelve..." (*I Corinthians 15:3G-5*).

However sticking only to the synoptic gospels, we do not know much more about the lot of Peter in the days after the resurrection. In fact, Matthew is totally silent about Peter. But clearly in Mark and Luke, Peter was a privileged witness of the resurrection in the continuation of Peter's primacy given to him before the passion as his destiny, no matter what his attitude and betrayal during the passion of Jesus might have been. He is forgiven, re-integrated and confirmed as primacy by Jesus himself. *No other person could have been responsible for this..*

John is much more explicit in this regard and in the double memoire that he has kept regarding the pascal experience of Peter, he will clearly mark his return into the project of Jesus in relation with his church. According to the fourth gospel, Mary Magdalene went alone to the tomb the morning of Easter. Finding it empty, she came back to "Simon Peter and the other disciple whom Jesus loved and said to them: 'They have taken away the Lord from the tomb'..." (*John 20:1-2*).

We know the rest. Both disciples decided to verify the words of Mary. The second beloved disciple ran faster than Peter, arrived first and observed the abandoned linens but did not enter. It is Peter who enters first to verify and only then does the other disciple enter: "he saw and he believed" says the gospel. And "the disciples went home" (*John 20:8,10*).

In the fourth gospel chapter twenty presents the event of Peter and the other beloved disciple at the tomb and chapter twenty one repeats this history but with a different nuance: "After this, Jesus manifested himself to his disciples again on the shore of Lake Tiberius" (*John 21:1*).

For our knowledge of the person of Peter, these two chapters are indispensable even if after the initial visit of Peter to the tomb, nothing more is said of Peter there and is only in the group of eleven to whom Jesus appears (*John 20: 19-20*) and before he sends them on their mission (*20:21-23*) and then is recognized by Thomas (*20:24-29*).

Chapter twenty one manifests the additional character of Peter according him a special place. The chapter starts with a catch of fish in which Peter participates (*21:3*) with Thomas, Nathanial, the two sons of Zebedee (James and John) and "two other disciples." At the end of a night in which they caught nothing, the resurrected one appears to them by provoking a sort of miraculous catch (*John 21:3b-6*). Having difficulty drawing in the net because of the multitude of fish, the disciple whom Jesus loved told Peter "it's the Lord" (*21:6b-7*). Peter jumps in the water to join Jesus and to drag in the loaded nets (*21: 7b-11*).

After the breakfast prepared by Jesus in which all participate, Jesus addresses Peter personally with a triple question: "Simon, son of John, do you love me more than these?" To which is joined "Feed my sheep" (*21:15-17*).

We know the pain felt by Peter by the insistence of Jesus to his triple denial of Jesus during the passion must correspond to the triple confession of his love which is *now without ambiguity, no restriction.* It's pure and simple, no boasting, no additional manifestation. And Jesus recognizing his sincerity remarks about the death Peter will undergo to glorify God, that is, as a martyr by which he will follow Jesus to the end. The final "follow me" evokes martyrdom and the mission of Peter to feed Christ's sheep. *Jesus does not ask this of any other disciple, not even of the beloved disciple. Only Peter:* "Feed my sheep.'

Here more than in any of the last chapters of the synoptic gospels, Peter sees himself invested with all that Jesus progressively conferred on him in the synoptic gospels before he passes starting from the changing of Peter's name.

In this sense, this chapter of John also deals with the distance Jesus establishes between Peter and the beloved disciple: "If I wish him to say until I come, what is that to you?" (*21:22*). The curiosity of Peter with regard to the beloved disciple was not satisfied. The essential for both is elsewhere.

CHAPTER XIII
EASTER

Easter is the celebration of passage. It is first of all a passage of God into the life and death of men. The word 'passage' is present throughout chapters 12,13,24 of *Exodus* which recounts the going out of Egypt by the chosen people, the passage through the Red Sea (sign of death) and the murderous passage through the desert. In the final analysis, it is God himself who passes with his people. We all dream of passing through life without failure, pain, obstacles, tragedies, sickness, worry, agonies. But Scripture insists on the fact that it was necessary for Christ to rise from the dead, from among the dead. Because death is our greatest problem, it seems to deny our life but it must be passed through. But our new life is not a simple continuation of our life here below. It is beyond death. In other words, we simply do not know what this new life is because nothing in our experience can be compared with it. The resurrection of Christ, if it remains the central affirmation of faith, remains and will always remain an enigma for us. Our own resurrection as well.

If God who is life itself passes into the life of man (the incarnation), our death must be overcome. There is absolutely no connivance between God and death. This passage of God takes us into an exodus which is a new birth. Our first birth is not denied, it is confirmed and accomplished. That first life was as it were a promise of life and the promise is held in an indiscernible manner. Paradoxical because that life obliges us to render our self deaf to the message of death, to that which the spectacle of God tells us of our precarious condition. The passage of God, Creator of life and freedom, culminates in the pascal enterprise of Jesus and that from the very beginning. Easter reveals to us a hidden mystery from the beginning of the world, a reality at work, active throughout the passage of history: the victory of life over death. We stake our existence on this: that belief that God, the foundation of our being, is the God of life and not of death.

Clearly we celebrate a central event, the resurrection of Jesus, but this event is paradigmatic (an exemplary and significant fact) of our own adventure on earth. Already the exodus of Israel presaged and illustrated it with their access to freedom. That is why the pascal vigil is replete with biblical passages of all the biblical figures of our creation and liberation. With Jesus the drama of this freedom and liberation is done, accomplished, but Jesus himself tells us "Where I go you cannot come yet but you will follow later" (*John 13:33,36*). We must live by having before our eyes the living Christ, the firm promise and anticipation of our own resurrection. Such is the foundation of our hope, the basis of our faith in life. Before our eyes? In reality, there is nothing to see, only to believe the word. The Gospel of John tells us that the apostle upon arriving at the tomb "he saw and believed." What did he see? Emptiness, an absence, but also an open tomb.

No tomb is sufficiently closed, so firmly closed to stop and halt the life of God. He is risen.

II.

The second Sunday after Easter captures the unbelief and surprise and anger of us all (*John 20:19-31*) in the person of Thomas the Apostle. "Unless I put my fingers in the nail wounds and my fist in his side, I will not believe." That's each one of us in the silence and frustration of faith. No God to respond to anything, to pain, to suffering, to sickness or dying, to our loneliness, to injustice and hardness, to avalanches and plane crashes, to accidents and indifference - the silence of God is overwhelming. We all want to scream with Thomas something like this: "You bastards, stop bothering me with all this good news that breaks my heart because it isn't true in my life. I followed him, ate with him, saw him die like a criminal nailed upon a cross by those damned Romans, without pity, without shame. I even saw his nakedness mocked by our so called leaders, curse them all! For what? For what? For being good? For being kind to all that damn screaming mob that he freely healed and did only good? They killed him for his goodness. People are no damn good. And look at me, how I ran! We all said how brave we were going to be and when the time came to stand up for him, what did we do? We ran. We are responsible for his death and now you give me this nonsense about his being alive. When some one dies, he's dead, dead, dead. He's dead and you never see him again. That's it, you stupid jackasses. I don't know whether to beat you or kill myself. I know I'm no good but here you are telling me you've seen him. You're worse than bastards, you're cruel and mean. Just leave me the hell alone. You want to tell that ghost of yours something? You tell him I'll believe when I grab his hands and put my finger in there and shove my fist right in that side where I saw that damn soldier lance him. O.K., that's your answer to your ghost or spirit or whatever the hell your sick minds saw. Now I don't want to hear about that Jesus again."

That's the answer each one of us wants to give anyone who tells us that one we saw die is now alive. Even today the announcement of the resurrection does not revive our faith as it engages and calls out to us for belief. Each time that resurrection is announced, it is a call to our faith as it was to Thomas on that first Easter evening. In fact Scripture presents the resurrection as a trial of

55

faith, the decisive test of our faith. It's all there or it is nò where. It is true or we are the most stupid of men for we are as yet in our sin with its promise of death, of body and of soul.

In all these recitals of the encounters of Christ which are of different literary genres, the first reaction of the disciples is of course one of unbelief, incredulity, fear when they finally recognize him (strangers, gardeners, beach bum, cook).

In *Luke 24:37* even when they were conscious of the new life of Jesus when the disciples saw him, they were seized with fear and took him for a ghost. To believe is not natural nor does it go of itself. For Paul, the announcement of the resurrection is the very touch stone of faith: to believe is to believe in the resurrection, in the God who raises the dead. It is the resurrection that separates, sorts out believers and non believers. It's that simple. Not to believe in the resurrection is to be without God (*a-theos*) in this world (*Ephesians 2:12*). Without the resurrection what good is God? For man, he is nothing. For the Christian, it's that serious. It is the basis, the foundation, the very skeleton of Christian faith. Without it, our faith is a lie. That's serious.

If Christ is not resurrected, Jesus may be a prophet, a wise man, a guru, a famous teacher of morality among others (Moses, Mohammed, Confucius, Buddha, Gandhi, Tao, etc.). But nothing more. The Gospels and the Bible would be interesting documents for ethnology, the history of religion, psychology, morality etc. but would not and did not intervene in our destinies. We would be as yet all alone in an alone universe in an alone world. The intervention of God into our history is not a sort of guided missile of this history of who and what we are here and now. If no resurrection, there only remains a cruel God, manipulator of men or a far away God, a clock maker, a "thought of thought" who takes no interest in men once he has set the whole universe in creation and in motion. We could then all become pantheists or deists for whom nothing is of concern to God. We would be really without God in this world.

The whole edifice of our faith is built on the resurrection. Period. "If Christ be not risen, vain in our preaching and vain is our faith" (*I Corinthians 15:14*).

But we must repeat this over and over again. We affirm the resurrection but we are incapable of saying exactly what it is. When the earliest Christians asked Paul, "How will we rise?" he responds with a metaphor, a "trace" in the words of Dante: "That of a grain which dies and generates wheat" (*I Corinthians 15:35-38*).

John 20:19-31 insists on the marks of the nails on the body of Christ, even on his resurrected body to emphasize that this new body is not a ghost but is in a real but unknown way related to and is the same as, that body of Christ which was crucified on the cross: it is the same body but glorified whose meaning we are unsure of. This underlines that the Jesus of the resurrection is no longer the Jesus of before Easter even if it is the same Jesus, the same person. It is he who has passed by death and yet still guards the stigmata of history. Thus in the book of *Genesis*, Jacob is struck on his side, crippled forever, from his struggle with the angel who is really God himself (*Genesis 32:23-32*). Afterwards, his name is changed to Israel, strong against God. For Jesus, the resurrection is not just a simple brush with death, but as we have said, it is a going *through* death. The Jesus of today is not an ethereal being, antiseptic, spiritual in the sense of abstract being. The whole history of Jesus from the first day remains present in him; even the whole history of Israel representative of all human history.

Thus it is for us: what we live and traverse remains living forever in us. Even in the resurrected life of Jesus in which we shall share.

CHAPTER XIV
THE RESURRECTION OF CHRIST: YES OR NO
THE ONLY REAL QUESTION IN LIFE

To believe in God, in the divine, in the supernatural, does not make us Christians. Paul goes much further: he establishes an equivalence between "being without Christ" and being "without God in this world" *(Ephesians 2:12)*. For if we do not have God in this world what concern is it of ours that there is a God outside of this world? For Paul, and from the logic of all his epistles, all faith is completely dependent upon the resurrection of Christ: if Christ is not risen, God has not intervened in this world in favor of life. If God has not intervened, the whole biblical enterprise which is directed towards Christ falls into complete insignificance. The God who does not intervene, who does not manifest himself as God with us, has no importance for us. We can completely ignore him and we are left with no hope, no future. The "thinking thought" separate from the world who was God in Aristotle is simply absurd and of no importance existentially to any of us.

That is why the compliment of the word "to believe" is always (in the epistles) the resurrection of Christ. He who believes, believes in this God who raised Christ from the dead, who intervened in our history, in a special place and time, to a particular people. The formulas are familiar: "If Christ is not risen, vain is your faith and you are as yet in your sins *(I Corinthians 15:17)*. "If the dead do not rise, let us eat and drink because tomorrow we die" *(I Corinthians 15:33)*. The resurrection becomes not only the touchstone of faith but the stone of scandal, the last test, the last temptation. Far from coming to comfort the faith of his disciples, the resurrection demands that faith: before this stupendous good news, will the disciples show themselves believing or unbelieving? The cultivated Greek of Athens listen intently to Paul when he spoke of God "in whom we have our life, our movement and our being." But as soon as he spoke of the resurrection, almost all of his audience left

58

him and only a few remained. We are reminded of the double edged sword of *Hebrews 4:12-13* which leads to what is most hidden in the hearts of men. Before the resurrection, it is not possible to waiver: for or against the God of life, he who overcomes our death. There is no *via media*, there is only 'yes' or 'no.'

There are many other texts in Scripture. *Acts 23:6-10* and *25:13-23* where Festus, the Roman magistrate reveals the reason for the imprisonment of Paul: "The accusers [of Paul] presented themselves and charged him with many crimes of which I found none. They had a great discussion with him on their religion about a certain Jesus who died and whom Paul affirms is alive." Such is the core of the problem, always the same question that is constantly posed to each one of us. Is this event real or a figment of our hopes and desires?

If to believe means to believe in him who rose from the dead, we can ask ourselves about the faith of those who preceded Jesus, in particular all those men and women of the ancient alliance, representatives of the whole of humanity. Abraham was the prototype. He was the "father of believers," the faithful exemplar who inaugurated "the people of believers." Did he have an authentic faith without believing in the resurrection? In *Romans 4:17-25* Paul says of Abraham that he believed in God as the one who gives life to the dead and calls those who are not, into existence. Abraham manifested this faith when he believed in the birth of his son Isaac even when he was old and decrepit and even though Sarah, his wife, was advanced in age. From these "dead bodies" God caused to spring forth a new life, for with God, nothing is impossible.

The epistle to the Hebrews takes up the figure of Abraham when he ties up Isaac for sacrifice. He was willing to give his son up to death, knowing that God was fully able to raise life in his promise. "God is so powerful that he can raise the dead. Thus he received back his son who was a figure." Of what? of whom? Of Christ risen from the dead, clearly.

Faith in the resurrection then is in the biblical recital, hidden, in figures from the beginning. This could not be done unless the work of the resurrection was already at work, hidden and active from the beginning of the world. It was there, active but hidden, not yet revealed. Thus the formulas in Paul in *I Corinthians 15:12-15;* "If there is no resurrection of the dead, Christ is not risen." Paul speaks as if the resurrection preceded Christ. A reality which affects the whole universe and is revealed in Jesus. Jesus himself put it this way: "Have you not read what God said about the resurrection of the dead: I am the God of Abraham, the God of Isaac, the God of Jacob? God is not the God of the dead but of the living." *(Matthew 22:31-32)*.

By this formula of the God not of the dead but of the living, Jesus corrects the image which men have of God. "Correct" is a weak word. He inverses the image and completely subverts it. The words of the serpent in the garden signifies that in man there is a suspicion of God, a distrust. He is avaricious, not generous. *Confronted with physical death, man chooses to believe in death.* He dies from that belief. This destructive defiance can be said to be original sin. From one point because it reflects on him who is our origin but also because it arises with our beginning; it affects the manner by which we receive being and life. It's a little like responding that it's too good to be true, there has got to be a catch somewhere. Fear of life, fear of God.

Scripture does not resolve this problem completely. For a long time God was seen as he who gave life and death. God of life certainly but also the God of death. It was clearly a case of surmounting a clear and ever present danger to man: death.

The resurrection of Jesus alone responds to the question posed in *Genesis 3*. The resurrection is the last word of Scripture, the last word of God, about God. Whatever comes later - including the final manifestation of Christ, can only be the deployment of the resurrection. God forever after appears as the gift of self to let us live, nourishment of our life, the use of death itself to bring about life. Much Christian language still views God in murderous images. Such formulas as "the death of your child is a test" - are awful. God enters our death to condemn it, to become a source of life. God does not produce death. If death exists in God, it consists in that death by which he gives his life that others may live.

The resurrection is revealed in Christ. There is found our hope, even if we don't fully understand the meaning of "risen from the dead." The Gospels put it his way: everything was started by a rumor circulated in Jerusalem. One of three condemned criminals on the Passover died but was alive, came back. The disciples of this crucified one were at the source of the rumor. What was their evidence since no one saw the actual event itself?

The first evidence is that of an empty tomb ("why do you seek the living among the dead. He is not here, he is risen" *(Luke 24:1-8)*. This empty tomb on the morning of Easter has been the subject of much speculation. Clearly that the tomb that was discovered empty does not constitute a proof of Christ's's resurrection. Mary Magdalene thought that someone had simply removed the body *(John 20:16-18)*. It was not a proof *but a sign*, appealing to faith. Taken literally, the passage would indicate that it was the same physical Jesus who was awakened and continued his life in space and time, just as before. This could not be because Jesus is now glorified. *The empty tomb simply means that death could not hold Jesus. Death is deprived of its fruit.*

Christian tradition has insisted more on the empty tomb than on the open grave. But all four Gospels speak of the large stone which was rolled away. The symbolism is clear: we are referred to *Exodus*, to exit. The resurrection takes the form of a birth from an empty womb which has given up its fruit *(John 16:21)*. Israel exits from Egypt (slavery and death) and wanders for forty years in the desert and finally exits the place of death to the Promised Land. It was the birth of a people. This is the authentic image of God: creator of freedom, the God of all birth. God is openness, genesis, the God of life, not of death.

Jesus appears and disappears and we cannot localize him. When Jesus disappeared to pray in the desert, the disciples could always find him *(Luke 4:5)*. After the resurrection, he is not there to be found at will. He renders his presence visible only when he wants. He is there and then he is not, he is the same ("he showed them his hands and his feet") but he is not the same. This signifies the new way of being "body" for which Paul invents the expression of "spiritual body" *(I Corinthians 15:44)*.

All this contradicts the naive belief of resuscitation as if Jesus just continued his former life. He is no longer "of this world." It is truly the same Jesus, but the disciples do not recognize him at first. Mary Magdalene sees him as the gardener *(John 20:11-18);* the disciples of Emmaus see him as a sojourner *(Luke 24:3-32)* and the disciples see him as "a spirit" *(verse 37)*. Jesus escapes their immediate recognition. What we call the Ascension has already psychologically begun. He is with the disciples in a mode of presence-absence, appearance-disappearance which signifies a new manner of being. The disciples however were wrong to see him as a "spirit" and the Gospels accumulate a whole series of details destined to show us that he is a body. In *Luke 24* "See my hands and my feet: it is truly me. Touch me, since a spirit does not have flesh and bone as you see that I have. And saying this, he showed them his hands and his feet." If this does not suffice, he asks them for something to eat. "And they gave him morsel of broiled fish which he took and ate in their presence" *(Luke 24:39-43)*. In *John 20:27* Jesus insists that Thomas touch his wounds.

That is why Christian faith professes "the resurrection of the flesh." The immorality of the soul is not the heart of our faith. We do not find this in the Gospels. Jesus truly dies, totally. And totally he is raised; but it is a life about which we can say little except *that it is* corporal in a way that completely escapes us.

II

Thus Christian faith looks to the resurrection of Christ in the flesh. It is therefore altogether unacceptable to preach the indignity of the body. There is an exaltation and glorification of the flesh. Even in the face of contrary Greek attitudes in some of the Greek Fathers of the Church.

"Flesh" in Scripture does not signify just "body" but the integral human person. If the Bible makes a distinction between body-soul in later redactions it never constructs its vision of man on this distinction. The Greek view has led us to confuse body with matter. But the body is matter penetrated by spirit. How could we communicate if we had no body? Whoever is deprived of his five senses would be absolutely helpless and incapable of a communion of love. That is why salvation which is ultimate communion with God-Origin-Father with nature and with other men, comes to the body, the flesh. The body of Christ was delivered up but then resurrected to new life and who is finally given to us as nourishment for a new life.

The resurrection of the body has another aspect. Our bodies are initially related to time. It is by time that we are temporal. Our bodies bear all that we have lived. *The same with Jesus who is not risen without the traces of his blessed wounds, so too we do not rise without the integrity of our past, our history.* At what age shall I arise? At all of them. My time is not lost but a time transfigured. "All that comes to the light becomes light" *(Ephesians 5:14)*. For God, nothing is destroyed, all is saved in the final perfection to which our lives are orientated, even unknown to us.

63

Our history is not a solitary history; it is a history with others. That is the way *we* are saved. Eternal life is communion. Only that is destroyed which cannot survive - what in our lives is an obstacle to communion: "Charity never passes away" *(I Corinthians 13:8)*. And charity is lived in and through our bodies *(James 2:15-16; John 3:17)*.

What cannot live? That which is not eternal: lies, untruth, evil, hatred, violence, greed, uncaring, murder, cheating, adultery, unfaithfulness, distrust, abortion, murder, fornication, theft and robbery, sexual perversions, in fine, all acts of injustice, impurity, faithlessness and uncharity. The eternal does not lie in them. If we are so penetrated with these, we may cease to exist at all. That is why it is so important by the grace of God to build up within us that which is eternal: the struggle for truth and to follow it once found, courage, responsibility, faithfulness in good and bad times, honesty, integrity, kindness, generosity, sexual purity, simplicity, mildness and humility, above all charity of which all the former are but participators in the latter. These alone will survive because they are eternal and because they belong properly to God.

For the *Acts*, Jesus showed himself alive and made many proofs of this: "appearing to them during forty days and speaking to them about the Kingdom of God" *(Acts 1:6)*. This time of apparitions is a no man's land during which Jesus gives proof of a disconcerting existence, at the same time in this world as well as beyond it. To what does this strange period respond? It resembles neither the time of Jesus on earth nor that which followed. By his resurrection, the human life of Jesus entered into the life of God. The Ascension only revealed what was already in the resurrection: it inaugurated a new regime. *Henceforth we will no longer see Jesus, only his disciples. So too, one no longer hears him, but that of his disciples (John 17:8). The words of God given to Jesus, Jesus has given to the disciples. They must be listened to.*

The time of apparitions where Jesus speaks of the Kingdom of God can be seen symbolically of the time in which we live. Everything has been given to us in Christ and yet we hold nothing with stability. We await, a new waiting for fulfillment and perfection. Israel awaited forty years in the desert as Jesus spent forty days in the desert in prayer before his public life. The number forty is symbol for a time of passage, change, conversion. It is symbolic of all human life on route toward its perfection. It is during these forty days in which our entire existence is covered in which we must find the truth of the resurrection, that of Christ and of our own and live it. *This lapse of time is given to us for the maturation of our faith.*

Resurrection of Every Day

For us, the resurrection is first of all a recital which we have received from the Apostles and from a believing people, the Church. As Paul says "faith comes through hearing" *(Romans 10:17).* Faith comes through a body, social and individual. Jesus in *John 20:29* declares blessed those who have not seen but have believed. The time of appearances has gone and there is nothing more to see, not even the empty tomb. Thus we cannot "prove" the resurrection but we can perceive some signs. As with every sign, they are an appeal to faith and mean nothing without faith. What are they?

All that succeeds, all that restores, all loving relationships, all the forms of peace which are concluded, every act of justice, love, compassion, every seeking for the truth, every rejoicing in the truth wherever found, every act of love and compassion - all these are the way to God and are all part of the resurrection, which go toward life and away from death and nothingness. Every time we escape some form of death from our division and hatreds, the hand of God is there. But there is a time when all signs disappear: the hour of the cross of Christ, the hour of our death.

This absence of sign, this symbolic victory of death is not the last word. It is simple delay, awaiting, terrain of hope. Faith is not content to simply decipher life in what succeeds in positive signs. It deciphers life-resurrection also in the image of death. In fact, it is there that faith awaits its perfection. Seeing Jesus die, the centurion recognized the Son of God *(Mark 15:39).*

Finally, it is our faith itself, the fact that we believe in Christ is the sign of the resurrection. And ours. This improbable faith, this impossible faith which is simply there, obstinately is placed in us. Work of God clearly, voice in us of the Spirit. By faith received we go forth from death which opens our tombs. For a new birth is given us by which God reveals himself as Father ("This day have engendered thee," *Acts 13:33).* The birth day of martyrs is the day of their birth *(Hebrews1:5, 5:5).* God in Christ has come to assume our human death. Because he has joined us in our death, all our deaths join his, the place of the resurrection. "We are dead with him, we rise with him" in Baptism.

In *I Corinthians 12:1-18,* Paul speaks of Christ and his members who are the Church. This new body of Christ is at the same time one and many. There is between the many members of Christ an organic communion. The Christ is the new body which the Spirit gives to Christ as he has already given him physical body. This new body is plural. We are all together the body of the resurrection. That is why the commandment of love occupies a central place in the New Testament. This imprint of the Spirit is in us by which all together we are made one. The resurrected Christ is all in all reassembled in him: "Jesus is resurrected in the Church" as well as "we, the Church, are reassembled in the resurrected Christ." We are in Christ and Christ in us *(John 17:2023).* It results that the Church, in its visibility offered to all, is itself the sign of the resurrection.

John 17:20-23 teaches us something else and makes more precise the manner in which the Church is sign. In *John* we see a compiling of two words that always go together: see-believe. It is the sight of Jesus and the signs which he performs by which men are led to faith. Jesus himself is the central sign who is given to us. "You have seen but have not believed." That is a constant reproach in the mouth of Jesus.

Now Jesus passes into the invisibility of God. Is there nothing more to see to call men to faith? We have passed from a regime of seeing to one of hearing *(John 20:29)*. But *John 17* gives us a new sign, obscure it is true, imperfect because it depends on our freedom in receiving the gift of God. "That they may be one as we are one...that the world may believe that it is you who have sent me." *It is our unity, our mutual love which becomes the sign of the presence of Christ among us and in us.* God has given all into our hands *(Genesis 1:28)*. His entire work, creation perfected by victory over the last enemy, death, is confided to us *(I Corinthians 15:20)*. By his resurrection Christ has been elevated above all mortal powers of division - all passes to our responsibility.

Thus the Church, a people cemented by love, is the sign and anticipation for the whole resurrected universe from which division and death have disappeared.

Thus speaking of the resurrection has conducted us to an exploration of all aspects of the Christian faith. Here is found the knot that holds the whole Christian enterprise together. Therein is included the presence and the activity of the Spirit who is the presence of God in us who becomes part of us, the interior dynamism who engenders in us the ability-capability of becoming one with others. The Spirit is the soul of the Church, the body of Christ. This dynamism is also very much ours but does not act mechanically. It is and must be activated by our "yes" to the true faith.

The whole of Christian faith is related to *relationship*. The "new man" born of the resurrection is *One*, reassembling all human beings, in the image of the one God. Because Christ is risen, our religion is a religion of person, of a living person because we are all related by and through the bonds of love and charity.

That is why the Christian religion is not first of all a morality, a list of things to do and to avoid. It is a relationship to a living person who joins us with himself and *eo ipso* with all others who believe and love and who recapitulates us all. *(Ephesians 1:10; 4:10)* Charity perfects the law. The Christian religion does not consist first of all in a list of things to believe. It consists in relationship to a living person to relate to, to love, in whom we place our confidence, our trust, our faith, our hope, our love. Dogmas have no other function than to explicate the person of Christ in whom and by whom we are related to God.

Our religion is not an explication or explanation of the world as a "system" destined to assure us of the coherence of the universe. Our religion is the living Christ, in us and in all making us one in love. *In him everything, even death, can make sense.* But it is not because of his "sense" that we go to him but because he is living. If he were dead except in memory, we would despair.

When I was a young priest, a woman came to the rectory where I was the pastor. Out of the clear blue, she asked for baptism. She was no more than fourteen. This was not the way things were done in those days. I asked her why she wanted to be baptized, whether she knew the terrible responsibility of becoming a Christian. After my long wind bag explanation, I asked her again, why? She said simply: "Because I know that Christ is alive and living." I turned my head and wept at her simple but powerful and trusting faith. No catechism lessons, no knowledge of morality or dogma, she went to the heart of Christian faith. I asked her if she loved Jesus and wanted to follow him with all her heart and soul no matter where it might lead. She answered, "yes." With a promise that she would come back for lessons, I took her to the church and baptized her in Christ Jesus. Such a person could not be refused.

How did she get there? She wasn't raised a Christian or a Catholic. It matters little because

68

she was led by the Spirit to confess the heart of Christian faith - "Christ is living." I baptized her with

water mixed with my tears that God had given me the grace to witness such simple and living faith.

CHAPTER XV
THE ASCENSION OF CHRIST

According to the special image used by the Gospel texts, Jesus was elevated into heaven, toward the "above." To this vertical movement there corresponds the horizontal movement of the disciples, sent from Jerusalem first, into all of Judea and Samaria and then to the very ends of the earth. Christ will no longer be visible on earth except in his disciples, "that they may be one so that the world may know that you have sent me" (*John 17:23*). Jesus who disappears definitely from human view, goes to inhabit heaven which is at the some time at the right hand of the Father and in his disciples. "We will come to him and we will make our abode in him." Thus heaven and earth, the high and the low are now reconciled with one tenant: the presence of God occupies all space. That was true from the beginning but henceforth men are implicated by their freedom into this presence. They have no longer "to look up to heaven." God is here through Christ in the disciples and in their human brothers and sisters.

The image of Jesus going up to heaven can hide an essential reality. We say that Jesus in accepting to die freely has conquered in him and for us all, the will to power, every pretension to impose good on men in spite of themselves. By raising Christ from the dead "God has established him above all powers and beings who dominate us whatever their name...He has submitted all things..." (*Ephesians 4:1-13*). Elsewhere Paul speaks about the submission of our enemies, of all the powers which harm us and where the last enemy, death, is conquered (*I Corinthians 15:25-26*). This power which raised Christ from the dead and made him Master of all that harms us passes into us. Such is the dynamism which propelled the disciples to go even to the ends of the earth, even to the shedding of their blood as witnesses.

The Gospel of Mark opens with the words "The beginning of the Good News of Jesus Christ,

Son of God." They are also the last words "They went forth to proclaim everywhere the Good News." The recital ends there, *opening to an unlimited future.* That is to say that the end of this Gospel is also a beginning and that we are, even today, before a continuous beginning. The Church also exists always to begin anew, beyond her wounds and failings. The promise of the miracles promised to the disciples can be disconcerting. That promise is simply a question of a symbolic illustration of the power given Christ and to those who believe in him, to surmount "all that is against us." We should be sanguine here: we know very well that the forces of nature continue to kill, that men of violence do not cease to kill and slaughter, that tyrants still impose their iniquitous laws by force and violence. Our victory consists in dominating all this but in faith. To elevate ourselves above all this because in the darkness and night, victory is ours. "So that by his death he could...set free all those who had been held in slavery all their lives by the fear of death" (*Hebrews 2:15*).

No matter the darkest hour, the agony, the pain, the imprisonment - even death itself - all that simply no longer matters. With the resurrected Lord, we have already overcome those powers of domination and death. In the midst of darkness we hear the cry 'Victory Is Ours.'

CHAPTER XVI
PENTECOST

Scripture expresses in diverse ways and in language of cultures long since forgotten, the desire among the most profound of every human being: to become like God (cf. *Genesis 3*). That is, to know and to do everything (which of course refers to a false image of God in any case) to exit our struggles and conflicts by realizing a unity of all men working on a common task. That was what the people building the Tower of Babel were doing in *Genesis 11*. It was an endeavor to rejoin the divine because the Tower went from earth to heaven. Through all these images we can see and understand that man wants everything, he wants the Absolute. The texts of *Genesis* tell us that this desire was put in man by God himself because he made man in his own image and likeness. But the legitimate desire became perverted by the temptation to take it by force, by man's own powers what God wants to freely give. We confuse unity with uniformity of men reduced to a unique mold (the same language of *genesis 11*). It was a false unity which did not respect differences and resulted in division.

God will put on the earth a new humanity: God and man will be one, men shall be truly reconciled, together they will be the image and likeness of the unique God. This is the meaning of Pentecost. By his Spirit, God comes to inhabit man and become in him a dynamism strengthening his freedom to lead him to the fulness of life. In place of the perverse and monolithic unity which we try and create by reducing others to the image which we make of the good, the unity which conserves and magnifies diverse languages and different ways of living and thinking. "Each one of them understood [the disciples] in his proper tongue" (*Acts 2:11*): the same message, the same Spirit, the same Christ but perceived differently. Are there not four Gospels? As for man and woman, the difference becomes the terrain of unity. Is this not this which we are saying when we speak of the truth? Thus the "curse" of Babel becomes finally a benediction by restoration of difference.

From all times, Christians have seen in Pentecost the birth of the Church (*Acts 2:1-11*). This is correct even if we find several versions of the coming and gifts of the Spirit. We read that Jesus in *John 20:19-23* gives the Spirit on the evening of that first Easter just as God breathed his spirit into the first Adam (*Genesis 2:8*).

God animates man by communicating to him his proper breath or spirit. This new man is at the same time one and many. It is "I" but in the exact measure that I accept to participate in one body with all my brothers and sisters. It is the Spirit who gives Christ this body which is co-extensive with all humanity and it is this same Spirit which animates and gives this body life. In *Galatians 5:16-25* Paul insists on the diversity of members of this body which is the Church, on their forms and different functions. It is not a question of difference of prestige, or dignity nor finally of power but of a harmonizing complimentarianism. In this body, what belongs to one member of the body belongs to all. It is the Spirit which realizes what we call the communion of saints. For each one of us, the Spirit is the presence in us, of the God of all. By this Spirit we are one with Christ and in Christ and with each other.

II.

The Spirit is imperceptible, hidden like the wind that comes and goes as it wishes. Most Christians have difficulty representing the Spirit to themselves. The Father, clearly as well as the Son. But the Spirit is subtle, evanescent. The reason is because he is one body with us and by that fact makes us all into one body, the body of Christ animated by the same Spirit. It is the Spirit who speaks through us, who comes down by his power, changes us, changes bread into the body and blood of Christ, incorporates us into the one body of Christ because he is the Spirit of Christ.. Above all, it is the Spirit who reassembles us all, who causes barriers to break down to unite us as one, who destroys the distance between us and the stranger. God is the unique Creator: each time we build up another, help another, love another, strengthen another, to make him exist - it is God who acts by us and in us. By the Spirit - called the 'Creator Spirit' - every time we love in truth - and how very difficult it is to love in truth - it is the Spirit of love (who is God) who lives in us and by us. All the love in the world is of God no matter who it is who loves. One cannot truly love without being moved by the Spirit to do so. It is not possible for us to produce love, we can only receive it, accept it and be willing to transmit it. We can give love only because we have received it from the Spirit because the Spirit has been given to us. By that fact, the Spirit becomes ours not in title of possession - we never possess God because God always possesses us - but as a permanent guest who is received into our souls, into our beings.

The Spirit, says Scripture, attains all extremities, reaching from eternity to eternity. That he fills all with his presence and joins contraries: the Creator and the creature, brothers who are enemies; masculine and feminine; all colors, races, ethnic groups - the races in all their diversity, strange mentalities, different cultures are united in the Spirit. All those who do "not speak the same

74

language" but who, however, are called to become together one body. Diversity, difference can serve as a terrain of hostility and division but in the Spirit they run together into unity. *Moreover, there can be no true love without difference.* Thus the Spirit has as it were a function to exercise within each individual as well as a social function. In each one of us, the Spirit creates the very possibility of communion with all and it is always the Spirit who is the unique Spirit who realizes the unique body of Christ in us all.

Pentecost according to *John 20:19-23* is much more discrete than the description given in *Acts 2: 1-11*. No tongues of fire, no wind, only the gentle breath of Christ in the upper room on that first Easter breathing on the apostles, bestowing upon them, the gifts of the Spirit. This gentle breath returns us to the creative Spirit of *Genesis 1:7* and the Spirit of God who animates Adam (*2:4*). Breath, Wind, Spirit are practically synonymous in Scripture when it speaks of God. In *John 20:19-23* we are in a scenario of creation, of the new creation, of the Spirit who is sent forth to renew the face of the earth. It is re-creation because it is the evening of the resurrection. The world begins again by the movement and the power of the Spirit. It is a world on the threshold of a new history which consists in overcoming - laboriously and painfully - our murderous divisions. The Spirit is given for exactly that - to unite us into a body of love - the body of Christ - where division, hatred and violence are definitively overcome. Does it really suffice to say that the Spirit is given for the remission of sins (*Galatians 5:16-25*)? Yes, in one sense: is it not sin, that is, our non love which impedes our unity? It is the Spirit, the Spirit of Christ and the Spirit of love who comes to us in that one mysterious body of Christ in which and by which our murderous divisions, hatreds and violence are overcome. We have only to say 'yes' to receive this precious and utter gift of loving unity who is the Spirit.   *Veni Creator Spiritus*

CHAPTER XVII
THE HOLY TRINITY

In the sciences and in philosophy we continuously discover more each day that the human person is totally relationship, or is better characterized by the more incisive word, 'exchange.' Exchange of chemical substances, exchange of knowledge with others, exchange in every area of life. There is nothing in us that does not somehow come from without. If we seek what underlies all matter, what is most fundamental in all matter, we come to the concept of rays of energy, energy fields, a metaphor which is exchange without being able to define clearly what is exchanged.

All this does not of course "prove" the mystery of the Trinity but we believe that all that exists is a reflection of God who created all that exists of which man is the summit and glory. If everything is exchange-relationship it is because what establishes us in being, what we call God, is in himself exchange and relationship in a way that is inaccessible to our reasoning powers. From his interior exchange "in God" flows the exchange or relationship of God with us. It is of the very nature of God to communicate himself (*defusum sui*) even if this communication is both necessary and totally free. That is why John's Gospel begins with "In the beginning was the Word", the place of communication.

In *Deuteronomy 4:32-32, 39-40* the emphasis is on a people, the unique relationship of God with Israel, on the "divine energy" put at the service of a people. A people, i.e., a whole network of relationships. The discourse is in the second person of the singular to signify the unity of the members of this people. The social and political relationship is also a form of "the image and likeness of God." The relationship of God with us is inscribed in all of our mutual relationships. St. Thomas says that Politics is the organization of charity. The exchange-relationship which God has with us which we call covenant or alliance is the source and as it were the model of our mutual exchanges. *That is why we are commanded to love as God loves.* It is in entering into this divine logic that we can "know God" which does not mean to comprehend in the intellectual sense of the word. We enter into the knowledge of God at once by accepting the Good News of what God has done for us and letting this revelation model and shape our lives. We discover the Trinity by receiving and giving the gift of God.

The New Testament shows us Jesus speaking to his Father as to another. At the same time, Jesus says "the Father and I are one." Both the Father and Jesus give us this Spirit. This Spirit is neither the Father nor Jesus because it is necessary for the Son to depart so that the Spirit can come and authorize us to address the Father of Jesus as "Our Father" "Abba" (*Romans 8:14-17*). Yet this Spirit has nothing of his own (*John 16:14-15*): he is one with the Father and the Son. All that which makes God to be God is found in each, circulates from one to the other and comes to us, spread forth in our hearts by the Spirit. In us and between us. Thus is revealed the unity of God and his unity with us and we with each other. *Humanity is called to unity and can unify itself because God is a unity in a plurality.*

We can say that God gives us his unity: "As you, Father, are in me and I in thee that they may be one also in us...I in them and you in me so that they may be perfectly one" (*John 17:20.23).*

Sometimes we have the impression that the mystery of the Holy Trinity is far from us, far removed from us, does not concern us. In reality, it is our very mystery of which it is a question. The mystery of the Trinity is also exactly our mystery.

SECTION III

CONSEQUENCES

CHAPTER XVIII
THE NEW COMMANDMENT

The death and resurrection of Christ inaugurated an absolute newness in the world ("*nihil novi sub sole*" "nothing new under the sun" is no longer true) for all of mankind since all men and women are subject to death. In other words, the good news for us all is that death does not have the final word in human history, neither individually nor collectively. This brings a profound joy to the human heart which is continuously darkened with the thought and reality of dread, the dread of inevitable death which confronts us at every moment of our existence. Death is sure but since we do not know the exact moment of that death, dread is the very horizon against which we live our lives.

Christians very early interpreted the resurrection event not only of God's approval of the mission and person of Jesus; but above all as the great sign and symbol of God's love for all men and women. The community of the beloved disciple tried in the first epistle of *John* to testify with the fruit of its meditation on the great revelation.

> "My beloved, let us love each other since love is from God and everyone who loves is a child of God and knows God. Whoever fails to love does not know God because God is love. This is the revelation of Gods' love for us that God sent his only Son into the world that we may have life through him" (*I John 4:7-10*).

Love here is at the center of all worship. The term is used some ten times as a noun and as a verb. God's love is first; it is he who freely took the initiative and his only command is that we love one another because all love comes from God, The proof of his love is the sending and gift of his own beloved Son. The meditation of John's community gives us this fact of faith: the commandment of fraternal love ("love one another") finds its source and realization in the insane or irrational or unimaginable love of God offered to all men freely, gratuitously while we are as yet sinners. God has loved us absolutely from the beginning in and by his beloved Son through whom all was created and in whom by the Spirit of Love we are sons in the unique Son.

> "Oh, Lord, we know that you love us because your Son has shown us that love. Therefore if it be pleasing to you, give us the grace of courage to love our brothers and sisters freely, gratuitously and for no other reason than they are your sons and daughters, both those that we love and those whom we do not love enough."

There is a second dimension of love which we should consider carefully.

> "My beloved, if God has loved us so much we too should love one another. No one has ever seen God, but as long as we love one another, God remains in us and his love comes to its perfection in us. This is the proof that we remain in him and he in us that he has given us a share in his Spirit. We ourselves have seen and testified that the Father sent his Son as Savior of the world. Any one who acknowledged that Jesus is the Son of God, God remains in him and he in God. We have recognized for ourselves, and put our faith in the love God has for us. God is love and whoever remains in love remains in God and God in him. Love comes to its perfection in us when we can face the day of judgment fearlessly, because even in this world we have become as he is. In love there is no room for fear, but perfect love drives out fear because fear implies punishment and whoever is afraid has not come to perfection in love" (*I John 4:11-18*).

Thus a new dimension of love is given: love which is seen with that which appears to be a contradiction: God no one has ever seen and those of us have seen! John the believer does not contradict himself. He testifies to his experience of faith by taking up the words of the first Christian community. The love of God is not and can never be an abstraction. It is seen first of all in God's Son and in the love of the brothers and the sisters. He who has faith in the Savior of the world is inhabited by God - this is the confession of faith of the community. This proclamation is given in other words as well, all of which are synonymous: to see, to believe, to testify, to know.

"Lord we believe in you and yet we are divided. We *believe* in you for us and we are still torn. Forgive us and teach us to love."

What then changes in the life of one who truly believes in the resurrection?

> :"Let us love, then because he first loved us. Anyone who says 'I love God' and hates his brother is a liar since whoever does not love the brothers whom he can see cannot love God whom he cannot see. Indeed, this is the commandment we have received from him, that whoever loves God, must also love his brother.
> Whoever believes that Jesus is the Christ is a child of God, and whoever loves the Father loves the Son. In this way we know that we love God's children, when we love God and keep his commandments. This is what the love of God is: keeping his commandments. Nor are his commandments burdensome, because every child of God overcomes the world. And this is the victory that has overcome the world - our faith" (*I John 4:19; 5:1-4*).

The answer to our question is given by John. To believe has and must have an effect on our lives, on our actions. If someone says: I love God and has hatred for his brother, he is a liar. Faith in Christ is intimately related to love of the neighbor. In fact, it is impossible to separate the two because they are one love. To love God implies to love those whom God loves, that is, those who are born of God. How is this so? By keeping his commandments which can be summed up in one commandment: to love God and the neighbor as oneself. There really is no other commandment.

> "Lord, render our testimony honest and coherent. May our acts and words be true when we try to stutter some words on evangelical love."

CHAPTER XIX
THE REDEMPTIVE ACT OF CHRIST

The essence of the redemptive act, the atonement of sin, the pleasing sacrifice to God (if one wants to still use these words which have a checkered history) is the voluntary submission of Christ to the violence and murderous injustice of man and who thereby taught us the supreme lesson of who and what God is in the very ignominy and humility of the infamous gibbet of his cross. Namely, that God is love and pardon, that the obedient and loving Son put man's hatred and violence to death forever by not responding even to injustice and so, by not passing it on he absorbed that hatred and violence into his very death in his utter and complete surrender to the incomprehensibility of God. Christ thereby destroyed hatred and violence, the producers of death, once and for all in his suffering and death. Therefore God raised him from the dead forever conquering death and its source, hatred and violence. The redemptive act resides there.

One should carefully note that in the midst of the murder of the most holy and just man who ever lived ("who among you can convict me of sin?"), God's response is not counter violence or vindication or condign punishment of evil men who put Christ to death but pardon and love. God's response to evil/murder/violence on the cross against his only Son, is pardon, mercy and love. "Father, forgive them for they know not what they do." That is the supreme act of God's forgiving mercy *right in the midst of the greatest evil and violence.* That is the redemptive act, the act of reconciliation, the free grace of accessibility to God for all men in and through his beloved Son on the cross. The nadir of human evil is met with the apogee of God's forgiving love right there on the cross. Divine paradox.

Where we are, he was; and where he is, we will be if we die to sin, that is, to the hatred and violence in our lives, to rise in love forever. He followed us even to death, the death of a cross so that we can never again be alone even in the solitary act of death. Christ is with us every step of the way so that he alone, of all human beings who have ever walked the earth, could say "be not afraid" because I have overcome the world, I have overcome death, the last and final enemy of man. If we have died with Christ to hatred and violence then we will rise with him; what then do we have to fear any longer? Suffering, loneliness, death? That is why of all men, Christ alone could say to his disciples on that first Easter evening, "Peace be with you." "And he showed them his hands and his side." It is the same Jesus who walked and talked with them. It is not a ghost or a phantom or an illusion or an image or a projection of their dreams. It is the same Jesus who was crucified and who now lives in their midst but in the invisibility of God to whom he has now returned but who thereby is with us until the end of time.

He could tell us "not to be afraid" and have peace because of all men, he alone tasted death and overcame death. He is alive. We worship a Jesus who is not a memory or an example or a model but a real live person who tasted, suffered and died and who now lives, having conquered death once and for all. Of what could we possibly be afraid any longer?

We never need fear anything again no matter what befalls us in life. Christ is with us in life and in death. Christ came not to explain suffering nor even to eliminate it; he has come to bear it with us, to overcome it in his person, to assure us that God loves us and that the only thing that remains for us to do "until he comes" is to remember his example and serve and love one another in word and in deed. Thus the parting words of Jesus.

> "By this shall all men know that you are my disciples that you love
> one another."

> "As long as you have done it to one of these the least of my brothers,
> you have done it to me."

83

"You know what I have done for you? You call me Lord and Master and so I am. But if I have washed your feet, how much more must you wash each other's feet? I have given you an example."

He has not left us orphans but has given us his Spirit to be with us all days even to the very end. It is the Spirit of Christ who teaches us to love even as Christ loved. Jesus left that small band of followers called 'church' assembled in Christ's name and whose soul is the Spirit of Christ who must love one another serve one another so that the world will know that Christ has come. How will it know this? Because his followers live by an entirely different ethic than that of the world. They live only by the ethic of non violence, forgiveness and love.

CHAPTER XX
TO SEE, TO BELIEVE THE TRUE SHEPHERD: John 20:29

We know that in the Gospel Of John the words *you have seen but have not believed* appear often. To see Jesus and the signs he performed was sufficient for men to believe that he came from God. There is something strange here because the whole of Scripture is suspicious of a faith that demands to see miracles and other supernatural phenomena to prove that God is with us. True biblical faith comes from *hearing*. It consists in believing and accepting the word of another rather than demanding proof. Otherwise what we are really doing is tempting God by forcing his hand to do miracles so we may believe. *Throw yourself down for it is written that he has given his angels charge over you that you not stumble over a stone. You will not tempt the Lord your God.* Thus the meaning of *John 20:29: Because you have seen you believe. Blessed are those who have not seen and have believed.*

The time for seeing when Jesus was on earth is gone but he will return. Compare *What we have seen with our eyes and touched with our hands* of *I John 1:1* with *We shall be like him because we shall see him as he is (I John 3:2).* For the present we are in the time of belief without seeing and that is why miracles, apparitions, healings, etc are of very little importance to the faith.

John 20:30-31 tells us that the signs recounted in the Gospel have been written *that you may believe.* In other words, our faith is the acceptance of a recital, of a word that has come down to us through the centuries back to those who saw and touched these central events. Faith in this Jesus *that you love without seeing him, in whom you believe without yet seeing him (I Peter 1:3-9).* Jesus has joined the invisibility of God. Thomas the Twin, our twin because he refuses to believe without seeing. Jesus bends to his demand, the indulgence of God to his weakness out of love before the weakness of our defiance. It is remarkable that Thomas is invited to put his hands into the wounds and into he side of Jesus, to verify the signs of death. What this means is that Thomas sees that Christ was crucified (remember the disciples had all fled and were not witnesses of the execution of Jesus) and that he is now *alive*.

At the same time Thomas' case illustrates perfectly man's sin, namely disbelief and defiance before the word that says that God is love. Thomas does not believe on the word of another that God is the God of life, that God is that God of love, that God is the God of life and not of death. The scene before Jesus and Thomas is a scene of pardon, of absolution. Jesus and through him, God overcomes man's sin. Jesus comes to say to his disciples who had all abandoned him at the hour of need now have the power to forgive and retain the sins of man. In Thomas, Jesus remits the fundamental sin of defiance. The power to remit sin would be illusory without the power to retain sin but Jesus shows that only the power to pardon is to be exercised. If men can pardon one another, it is only because they themselves have been pardoned. All this is a new creation: the breath of Jesus on his disciples is the breath of God who originally animated and gave life to man in *Genesis 2:1-8*. He gives the disciples the power to give life by the remission of sins in his name.

God in Jesus is never absent from our lives even when we go seriously astray, even when our sins drive us to sadness. We can find in our world many signs of God's love but they cannot be the foundation of our faith: they speak to those who already believe in the Word. *Luke 24:13-35* speaks to those who have never seen Christ as the disciples on the way to Emmaus. We have three pillars of faith: Scripture (*v.27*), partaking of the bread (*v.20)* and the community (*vs.33-35*). A living community, a community which shares the bread in memory of Christ, a community that continuously reads the Scripture and is nourished by it.

Above all, we must believe in life and not in death. Emmaus recounts our own spiritual journey. The two disciples insisted on believing in death rather than life - we are they. There is between them (the same as we) hesitation ("we had hoped"). They believe that Christ was dead (they were right) but they remained there among the dead. Some women came telling that he was alive. A faint hope: is this possible? They themselves had not seen the resurrected one, neither did we. Both they and we must establish our faith as a recital which the woman spoke of. But our faith is weak - we must constantly come back to it.

One of the major themes of the Gospels is the going beyond human violence. In fact, sin consists in enslaving others, making them do our will, using them, violating them. Finally to murder them. Scripture rehabilitates the victims of human violence, all those whom we sacrifice and kill for good reasons, including economic reasons. *Acts 2:14, 36-41* speaks to us about the rehabilitation of Jesus: *This Jesus whom you crucified, God has made him Lord and Christ.* If God has rehabilitated Jesus by destroying those who injure and crucified Jesus, he would have in turn made further victims "for good reasons." To combat murder by murder only consolidates and promotes violence: *Covered with insults, he does not insult; filled with suffering, he menaces no one (I Peter 2:20-25).* Jesus did not pray his Father to send legions of angels. *He killed sin (violence) in his proper flesh by returning love for hate.* Against sins, God has only non violent arms, one weapon: pardon and mercy. It is pardon which puts violence to death.

John 10:1-10 speaks the same thing about the shepherd. It opposes those who come to pillage the sheepfold (*thieves and bandits*) who desire only to steal, kill and destroy (*v.3*). Coming in and out of the sheepfold is the sign of freedom because we are free men with the freedom Christ has earned for us. He has set us free from sin and *therefore* we are free. The true pastor comes that men have life and have it more abundantly. The pastor precedes the sheep, gives his life for the sheep (*v.4*) as the cloud preceded the Israelites in the desert which was really the divine presence. Jesus goes before us to the very end, to death itself, the death of a cross. The sheep follow the shepherd freely, voluntarily and not by instinct because there is an intimate relationship between Jesus and them. The time of the false shepherds, the thieves who use and devour the sheep is not over. Christ is without power, without prestige of power and force - will he find men to follow him in a world full of rapine, greed and murder?

Many Christians do not want to be likened to dumb sheep, passive to the conduct of a shepherd who alone knows best, decides, gives orders, etc. But this is precisely what the Gospel does *not* say, does *not* hold. Clearly Christ opens the door to salvation by his glorious death and resurrection and he *is* the door to green pastures (salvation). But the sheep enter and go out freely. The sheep and the lamb are not the symbols of a people led by the nose but a *figure of non violence*. *Men of blood and violence cannot follow Christ*. They lack the relationship with him. The relationship between pastor-sheep is not one of constraint or of authority in the usual meaning of that word. The terms employed in this text are *knowledge, listen to my voice (v.4), to call each one by name, whoever is of the truth hears my voice (John 18:37)*. In each one of us the life that wants to live in truth recognizes in Christ the way, the truth and the life. In following Christ, we are not abandoned but we are liberated for life, not for death which is the way of the world.

CHAPTER XXI
THE GREEKS WHO WANT TO SEE JESUS
John 12:20-33

In the time of Jesus, there were those who were sympathetic to Jews. They were sometimes called "Greeks." In *John 12:20-33* we see them come up to Jerusalem not to celebrate the Passover but on the occasion of Passover, to "adore God." They approached the disciples who then approached Jesus. When we say 'Greeks' we immediately think of the classical opposition between Jew and Greek (Gentile), members of the chosen people and strangers to the alliance. The gospel specifies Phillip as the intermediary between Jesus and the Greeks because he was from "Bethsaida in Galilee", Galilee which was the Galilee of the nations which was despised because those Jews cohabitated with Greeks.

John clearly indicates that while salvation comes from the Jews (*John 4:23*), the indication is that strangers are also about to be invited into the heritage of Israel. Salvation must attain the ends of the earth. We should also note that the Greeks come to Jesus by the intermediary of an apostle *and not the reverse*. Jesus "draws" all men to himself. Jesus is the respected opening of People's freedom to come or not, as they see fit. This respect for individual freedom is as much a lesson for us today as it was during the time of Jesus.

The Response of Jesus

At first glance, Jesus' response is disconcerting. He does not say 'welcome' or anything of the sort. He seems to be speaking beyond the Greeks, about something else. Jesus speaks of 'glorification., of 'a grain falling to the earth', of 'the hour which has come' from which Jesus wants to be delivered - evidently the hour of the pascal mystery. It is then that Jesus will be glorified, that is, he will be revealed for what he is in the eyes of all. Note the opposition between "fall to the ground" (*V.24*) and raised up from the earth (*v.32*): glorification is done by humiliation and the revelation of love, *which is the very truth of Christ and of God which is brought about by events where hate abounds*. Jesus joins us precisely where we die from our fratricidal hatred and we must, on our part, rejoin him in the place where he comes to occupy: the question of life and death because the grain that falls to earth must die to bring forth fruit because who seeks to save his life will lose it. Paradox. The impossible desire to save our lives must lead us to give it *because we save only what we give*. Paradox.

The fruits of the pascal mystery are innumerable and incomprehensible: "but if it dies it yields a rich harvest." The response of Jesus to the Greeks - in spite of appearances - is perfectly in accord with the asking-question of the Greeks. The Greeks want to see Jesus but they cannot yet see him in his truth except in light of the pascal mystery. For now they can see only a miracle worker, a famous personage, a brilliant preacher-moralist, a compassionate messenger. It is a curiosity close to that of Herod (*Luke 23:8*). It is only when Jesus shall have been elevated from the earth that he will draw all men to himself. There in effect is where Jesus' identity as Messiah and Son of God will be manifest.

Then, says St. Paul, there will no longer be Jew or Greek because "the prince of this world will be thrown out" (*v.31*). Who governs the prince of this world? The spirit of division, of domination, the will to power which possesses men and marks them one against the other. Christ, the Son of God and Son of Man, will create this unity among men by renouncing all domination and violence and become the servant of love by accepting to be reduced to powerlessness: Jesus has "come to serve not to be served and to give his life as a ransom for many." What ransom? A ransom from all hate and domination because he will become the servant of love.

> "Anyone who loves his life loses it; anyone who hates his life in this world will keep it for eternal life. Whoever serves me, must follow me and my servant will be with me wherever I am."

CHAPTER XXII
THE RISK OF LOVE (*John 20:19-31*)

To love is to risk, to risk being broken, deceived, abandoned. That is why most people refuse to commit to love because it is so dangerous and devastating, if lost or deceived.

John ends the first conclusion of his Gospel (the second conclusion is Chapter 21) by saying that the facts and actions of Christ were narrated in his Gospel that we may believe in Jesus and by believing in Christ, we may have life in his name. There is a new birth, a re-finding of life. We must become conscious of the consequences for us of the resurrection of Christ. When Jesus rose from the dead, it is we who, by him and with him, rise from the dead. Pious discourse? Empty language? To go beyond cliches, we must understand what that means and what it demands. By the resurrection of Christ we have received a profound revelation: that God is love through and through. Easter is a sort of demonstration, of a proclamation destined for all men and women. We learn that God, the foundation of all that is, the truth of man, is love and consequently, life is given to us freely as Jesus gave us his life freely and willingly.

But Easter is not just a demonstration; it is also an appeal, a calling. An appeal to love, an appeal to do what Christ did in memory always of Christ. Yet this must pass by faith. Faith in Christ to that which Easter represents, the perfection of life itself. Clearly this faith is itself a gift, a given, but we must accept to receive it which is presented as a trial which is so beautifully narrated for us in the story of Thomas, the Apostle. Like him, we know of the resurrection of Christ only by testimony, by living witnesses. We must believe on the word. Therefore, Thomas is our turn, even if Jesus ceded to Thomas his desire to see and to touch. This desire of Thomas is also our desire as well but it will be satisfied only later because the route traveled by Thomas in this Gospel designates and describes the map of our whole life. In waiting to encounter Christ, we are under the regime of "believing without seeing." Paul said it best: "faith comes from hearing" (*Romans 10:17*). *Seeing gives us a knowledge not a believing.* Only hearing puts us in relation with him from whom we receive the Word. Seeing leaves us on the outside. Only hearing lets us in because it is received only in faith.

It is because we believe in the love manifested by Christ giving and taking up his life again for us *that we can risk to love.* Our love must be and is an echo of his love. As John put it, God has loved us first (*I John 5:1-6*). This is surprising because John gives this love in the form of a commandment. That is because love cannot be facultative: who does not love is not born of God, that is, we are not the image and likeness of the one who has created and founded us. To be image and likeness comes back to being created, to exist, to escape our nothingness (*Genesis 1:27*). And this cannot be done without our consent and freedom. However, it is not for us a simple question of imitation of God as Christ has revealed him: we are absolutely incapable of loving as God loves by the efforts of our will or by any work of ours. That is why Easter is not content to give us an example: it gives us a sacred force, a dynamic force to bring this about, the Spirit of God himself who is love who inhabits our hearts. Easter is accomplished in us only by Pentecost.

CHAPTER III
CHRIST THE KING

Scripture is ambiguous about royalty and kingship. God was reluctant to give Israel a king because God alone wanted to rule Israel. Nathan gave them Saul, then David, then Solomon- and they all ended up badly forsaking the law of God for wealth, power and pagan practices.

Daniel 7:13-14, Apocalypse 1:5-8 and *John 18:33-37* all speak of royal power. In reality, royalty begins in *Genesis 1* where man is invested with the lordship of all creation. The text of Daniel introduces a slightly different motive. The "Son of Man," the name which Jesus appropriates for himself in the Gospels, will dominate all people, all the nations and all cultures ("languages"). Paul takes up the theme of domination of Christ but it is not exercised over men. Christ exercises authority over thrones, dominions, and powers. He subjects everything that is contrary to our welfare as well as the last enemy, death (1 *Corinthians 15:26).* This reign of Christ also rules in our hearts individually but there is yet in our hearts the residue of sin and connivance with death which ruins the humanity in man. These are the powers and dominations. In short, Christ does not exercise power over man but over the enemies of man.

The dialogue between Jesus and Pilate illustrates well this royal ambiguity. Pilate sees in Jesus a pretender to political power or perhaps even religious power (they were the same in those days). The word 'King' did not have any other meaning for him. Jesus enlightens him: his disciples did not fight to free him or to forbid him from being taken. Pilate just doesn't understand and even we have difficulty understanding this. Why not get someone to free Jesus because we know he is innocent and just. We all like the happy ending when the good guy is saved by the cavalry from evil forces just in the nick of time. We hope the same thing for Jesus but it doesn't happen. That is because Christ's

93

power is over what divides men, over the power to have power over men. For Christ. to rule means to give his life for others, to be the servant of all while being the Master. He is Master of service which is expression of love. This is the truth of God and of man which Jesus gives witness to. It is a power, yes, but it does not resemble the power of this world. Christ reigns by the attraction he exercises over man, over truth. He exercises the power of truth and who is of the truth hears his voice. And all those who hear the voice of truth let themselves be led by Jesus.

This misunderstanding of Pilate has had its imitators in the history of the Church as well. At certain stages of the Church's existence, they easily thought that the reign of Christ was for all men to be under the pontifical power. Then the kingdom becomes a kingdom of this world. This triumphalism can be accompanied by violence both mental and physical. This kind of power no longer tempts us. We must be continuously or guard against this way of viewing power by always having before our eyes the example and image of the Son of Man having power over the inhuman, over what enslaves us. *"They will look upon Him whom they have pierced."* To turn to Christ, to look upon him, to go to him are all equivalent formulas. They speak to us of our adherence, our conversion to him whose life we have taken and who has given us life back in spite of our murder. This is the victory of the cross.

II

The words of Saint John are striking: "My kingdom is not of this world" (*John 18:36*), that is, Christ's kingdom is not of the same nature as the kingdoms of this world. This nature is different but, as we shall see, it has a relationship with this world. If the whole notion of *Christianitas* has disappeared, the dream of a Christian politics still threatens to turn the gospel into an ideology. What becomes of the freedom of the children of God, of the free assent to a call if one's action is inspired by the faith which takes the form of law? There is no Christian math or Christian science or Christian medicine. Is there then a Christian politics? Certainly there is a Christian way to give oneself to ones medical or legal activities but a diagnosis and remedies in both cases obey an antonymous logic.

In fact, politics should be considered with nuance and subtlety because there is performed a relation between man and communities. But as soon as we say *relation*, as believers, we encounter the gospel. The theologians of the Middle Ages said that politics is the organization of charity. But if the word 'charity' makes us afraid, then substitute 'solidarity.' But the "simply human" when it is truly human is already bearer of the divine. That is why unbelieving lawmakers and politicians can very well (even without their intent) perform a "divine politics." All that humanizes goes in the direction of God. The "elect" of *Matthew 25* are those who hear the words "it is to me that you did it" and they will be mightily surprised that in feeding the hungry, visiting the sick, defending prisoners and taking in strangers that they will be told then that it was in reality to Christ that they did it. The passage says nothing of religion or even believing in God. Very strange indeed. When anyone comes to the aid of those in need even without a properly religious motive, it is to Christ that they did it. That is scandalous to some.

All this should warn us against a triumphant interpretation of the royalty of Christ. Jesus speaks of his royalty only in the fourth gospel during his passion but he speaks in ambiguous terms (*John 18:33-38*). In the synoptic gospels (*Matthew, Mark, Luke*) Jesus speaks of the kingdom of God. The title of Christ is found only in the mouth of the disciples or demons. When Jesus names himself, he calls himself "the Son of Man" and he forbids his listeners to tell others of his royal quality. In fact, the theme of the royalty of Christ is found in Saint Paul and in disconcerting terms.

Our freedom is always exercised under conditions of limitation. We are under the influence even under the domination of a multitude of forces which escape our power: our genetic code, familial background, social and legal conditions which weigh upon us. Natural forces also come to lessen our freedom from intangible laws like gravity, earthquakes, floods and other natural disasters.

Paul recapitulates all this under these terms: "powers and dominations" or "elements of this world." This is not all. Paul sees the human person subjected to a law which is in part related to our very freedom, the law of sin with its corollary, death. Paul sees this law of sin as a sort of interior dynamic which is a parasite on our freedom to the point that it renders us powerless. The famous passage from *Romans* (*7:14-24*) "If I do what I will not, it is not I who do it, but sin which inhabits within me."

Does this mean that our freedom is totally neutralized? Certainly not but it must work its way through a jungle of pitfalls and it is successful only to the extent and by means of the liberation of our freedom bought by Christ. This is within us a connivance with the powers and dominations of this world which enslave us. Others speak of a culture of death, lovers of death (*Wisdom 1:16*). In the desert, the Hebrews who become free, didn't they regret the comfort of the slavery of Egypt (*Exodus 16:1-18*)?

These powers and dominations encompass all that is contrary to us from the cosmic forces to the arbitrary powers exercised by tyrants in passing law. "It will be the end when Christ restores the kingdom to God the Father, after having destroyed every principality, domination and power. For he must reign until he has placed all his enemies under his feet. The last enemy to be destroyed is death' *(I Corinthians 15;24-26)*. This text places Christ's royalty "at the end" which presupposes that we are not yet freed from hostile powers. "The last enemy is death" was destroyed on the cross. In what does our present liberation consist when Christ "rules from the wood" and *yet we continue to die*?

Not Of This World

Our first understanding of "not of this world" is the kingdom at the end of time. Eschatology. This has a certain valid meaning as we shall see. But there is another interpretation. The royalty of Christ is not exercised like that of other powers, the powers and dominations, which Christ has overcome. "You know that the pagans and chiefs make known their domination and the great ones, their power. Not so among you. On the contrary, whoever wishes to become great among you will become your slave" *(Matthew 20:25-26)*. These words are found in all the synoptic gospels. They announce the passion and it is at the hour of the passion that Jesus answers Pilate "you have said it. I am a king." But Jesus adds immediately, revealing in what that royalty consists and how that royalty is exercised which is not of this world: "For this was I born and for this I came into the world, to testify to the truth. Whoever is of the truth hears my voice."

Christ reigns by another sort of attraction. Men are not constrained or forced but *drawn* or *called*. Who draws them, who calls them? What is the truth? The truth is of man himself, the truth of humanity is man, the truth for which we have nostalgia because it is ours from the beginning, from the foundation of the world, from creation itself. Our truth of human beings, if it establishes us, is also in our future because our perfected nature demands an altogether other history: our total communion with God to whom we are drawn and called, the word 'called' underlying the absolute freedom of our response all along the way. Thus it is the reign of Christ because it is we who freely give ourselves to him when we come to choose to obey our truth.

The Reign Of The Cross

"Once elevated from the earth, I shall draw all to myself" (*John 12:32*). Certain authors translate this "I shall draw to myself all men." This "elevation from the earth" is often used by John to mean the crucifixion but seen at *the same time* as glorification. It is at that moment that he has nothing to draw men with (*Isaiah 53:2*) "that they will look upon him who they have pierced" (*John 19:37*). But the crucified one is just, the only one who is just, whom we have put to death without reason because of hatred of justice and love. In this sense, the cross exhibits the murderous folly of men, our sins fully revealed.

But this evil which is unmasked is only a half victory. The kingdom of God, the kingdom of Christ is not truly established, except by pardon, that is, by love which superabounds where sin has abounded (*Romans 5:20*). This superabundant love Christ has manifested all during his life and it is that which finally killed him. It culminates when Jesus accepts to submit to the murderous will of men, renouncing all power, all dignity, even his will to live. Thereby he dominates all that which sets us all against each other and assures the victory of love over death, the last enemy. For all those who accept to turn toward him, is opened an immense hope capable of drawing all men because it expresses our ultimate truth.

Yet the victory of the cross remains a story for us and its truth in our lives remains hidden.

We remain under the domination of the law, of laws, of powers and dominations, of cosmic forces, All this is solidified in death. But as we have learned, we believe, all this can be used if we let love superabound in our lives.

> "For I am convinced that neither death nor life nor angels nor principalities nor present things nor future things nor powers nor height nor death nor any other creature will be able to separate us from the love of God in Christ Jesus our Lord." (*Romans 8: 38-39*).

Like Jesus who on the cross used the worst to make life triumph, we now have the royal power to make ours the image and likeness of love from all that oppresses us..

Cosmic Royalty

What we have said can lead us to believe that Christ rules uniquely "over souls", reigning with him over evil powers. All that is in the private area, the 'spiritual' of the individual. This point of view should not be minimized but integrated into a more vast horizon. It retains its validity because the relationship of God with man is an affair of freedom and that freedom is within me, the sanctuary of the person.

That said, our relationship to God by Christ concerns and includes all the others, in space and time. That is why all the alliances of the Old Testament even if they were concluded with individuals (Noah, David, Moses, Abraham, Jacob) are concluded with a whole people. Beyond this people is profiled "the nations," those sister enemies which end up by entering into the heritage of the chosen people, distinguished from them but elected like them. The result is that the kingdom of Christ, the fulfillment of all alliances, takes on a political, social and economic character as we mentioned at the beginning of this article. Nothing that is human escapes Christ because everything human is from God.

The question which is posed - a difficult question really - is on the way believers are going to translate the substance of this faith in a pluralist society for which Christianity is no longer a referential point. Perhaps we should remember what the Jewish disciples of Jesus did when they established the church into the world. They renounced all that particularized them: food practices, sacrificial rites, circumcision. We must embrace all that goes in the direction of the human and refuse all that dehumanizes and goes in the direction of barbarism. How to do this? By collaborating with all men of good will. Without ever forgetting that the reign of Christ is installed by a call, an attraction, and never by action aiming at force and constraint - even in a legal sense. All this of course does not stop us from announcing Christ crucified and resurrected in whom every human person and the whole divine enterprise is expressed and concentrated.

CHAPTER XXIV
FAITH THAT GROWS (*Luke*)

"...he himself stood among them and said to them, 'Peace be with you.' In a state of alarm and fright, they thought that they were seeing a ghost. But said 'why are you disturbed and why are there doubts stirring in your hearts? See my hands and my feet that it is I myself. Touch me and see for yourselves; a ghost has no flesh and bones as you can see I have.' And as he said this he showed them his hands and his feet. Their joy was so great that they still could not believe it, as they were dumbfounded; so he said to them 'have you anything to eat?' And they offered him a piece of grilled fish which he took and ate before their eyes" (*Luke 24:36-43*).

Faith is always a difficult thing. We are disturbed that sometimes we have such difficulty in believing in the resurrection. We are not alone because the original disciples had to pass by the same route. We affirm the resurrection without knowing exactly what it is, that Jesus does not simply take up his life as had it before, that his way of being a living body escapes us which also goes for our resurrection (*I John 3:2*): "We are even now children of God (i.e. participants in the very life of God) but what we will be has not yet been manifest." We ought not to be surprised that our faith in the resurrection comes and goes, knows shadows and eclipses. In fact, I believe faith has been given to me and it is useless to multiply efforts to construct or reconstruct it. Let us have confidence in God that he will give us confidence. As in the Gospel, Christ himself will come to affirm our faith.

What do the disciples say? "It is true. The Lord is risen and has appeared to Simon" (*Luke 24:35*). The disciples who came back from Emmaus confirmed it. Truly, faith is there. And behold Christ presents himself: faith disappears to be replaced by fear. They do not recognize him and take him for a "ghost." When Christ comes into our lives, does not Christ seem strange and a stranger? He comes to disturb our routine of faith which seems acquired. All of a sudden we are not so sure. Here are the disciples in a state of terror. This shows us that faith is not possessed as an object once and for all. Like the manna in the desert, it is to be received day by day. We are put into a state of waiting and expectation, of permanent disponability and openness. That is the 'daily bread' which is ours which we cannot stock up under pain of rotting. Yesterday's faith nourished yesterday, today we must start again fresh, with a new faith because God is always new in our lives. This faith is life and life is characterized by constant movement.

There are those who are shocked to see Jesus eat in front of his disciples. A 'spiritual body' according to *I Corinthians 15:1-8* cannot easily absorb food. Let us be liberated from problems such as 'where does that food go.' Let us let go of the question of physiology and molecules. What the Gospel tells us is that the resurrected Christ is body. The body is instrument of relationship with the cosmos and with other men. The meal of the resurrected Jesus manifests and shows that he is not cut off from the world or from his own. His communion with beings of nature and the human world takes on unheard of dimensions. Christ is "all in all." There are many ways to be body and the body of the resurrection remains a mystery for us, but there is to be found the foundation of our hope. A hope that includes the destiny of all creation (*Romans 8:19-22*).

CHAPTER XXV
THE BIRTH OF THE CHURCH: *Acts 2:42*

"They remained faithful to the teachings of the Apostles, to the brotherhood, to the breaking of the bread and to the prayers."

Such is the description that *Acts* gives of that small group assembled around Peter after his first discourse to the Jews at Pentecost (*Acts 2:14-36*). This is in typical Luke style given in such a way as to give us a birds eye view of that period for which he gives us no details but does not want to pass over in silence. The most significant of these Lucan summaries are found in his Gospel in the pages of Jesus' infancy (*Luke 2:40*).

This summary in *Acts* is more precise and describes a series of original data which projects a precious light on the history presented. Clearly this summary composed by Luke is many years posterior to the recounted events. These years were filled with many novelties, experiences, reflected on or spontaneous - so that one can ask about the exactness of so brief a resume.

But to look at this summary more closely, we find in a few words that it furnishes a significant tableau of the community which was born at the earliest date after Pentecost. It was summed up in one phrase which enumerates four points all perfectly defined each in its proper domain. The text does not seek further development, estimating that all alone each word sufficed to evoke a reality already known but also that the way of presenting the community gives us an expressive image of the original totality worthy of singular attention. Each of these four points should be examined in their singularity.

The Teaching of the Apostles

This could be the teaching given by Jesus, gathered and transmitted by the apostles. This could also be the teaching which consists in presenting Jesus, in explaining his person and his mission. Both are the first outlines of what would become the Gospels: the tradition of Jesus and the tradition *about* Jesus. In any case, the first place given to this teaching is without doubt the sign that is the series of rituals and practices which make the originality of the new community, that is, the word and personage of Jesus occupies first rank and retains their attention.

But it is also clear that for the author of this little synthesis, access to Jesus, to his acts, thoughts passes through the apostles who were with Jesus. Very early, we find the cry of Stephen under thrown rocks, "Lord, Jesus, receive my spirit" which expresses the spiritual encounter with the person of Jesus and the experience of his presence (*Acts 7:19*). From the earliest days, the person and work of Jesus fixes the attention of the community and forms their hearts. But the certitude of the community as well as its faith *reposes on the witness of the apostles*. This is extremely important since this event took place long before the composition of the New Testament scriptures. In other words, the New Testament canon was written under the authority of the witness of the apostles which guaranteed its authenticity. The witness and therefore the authority of the apostles preceded and was normative of the canon of the New Testament which authentically translated the acts, words and teachings of Jesus.

Fraternal Communion

The word 'communion' here takes on its strongest and largest sense. It is much more than a profound sentiment, a relationship between hearts, a way of existing together in the world. It is more than a style of life or a common understanding of reality. The teaching of the apostles was something entirely different from a body of truths to be retrained and confessed but it was a way of committing oneself to the way of the apostles as they followed the teaching of Jesus. This does not mean that the truths were not authentic; only that they had to be lived as well as known.

104

This term furnished precious indications for the first Christian community. The relation which united then is very strong and very concrete - not adherence to a constituted organization, nor a personal commitment to promote a cause. This was clearly a visible dimension (the Apostles) but their role is first of all to assure the continuity with the person of Jesus and their authority is first of all that of their witness to the words and teachings of Jesus.

This communion is a lived experience together and also a partaking of the same type of existence. A more detailed summary later makes more precise how the sharing of resources in the community so as to leave no one in need would be done by the community (4:32-34).

The Breaking of Bread

The word of Luke whether at Emmaus (24;30) or at Troas (*Acts 20:11*) or in peril of the sea (27:35) designates at the same time the meal which reunited the community and the significant ritual which commemorates the last supper of the Lord. That a ritual so particular, so rapidly exercised and easy to do took such an important place, gives to the breaking of bread an exceptional meaning. We cannot say that it abolishes the value of the temple because in the same phrase the resume of *Acts* signifies that the disciples frequented the temple regularly and broke bread in their homes (2:36).

This paradoxical association is an evident sign that the early Christians always felt themselves to be members of the people of Israel and attached to its rites. They also give to the breaking of bread an equivalent value to that of the temple. Years later, the letter to the Hebrews will explain that the gift of his life offered by Jesus Christ on the cross surpasses by far the greatest sacrifices offered by high priests of the temple. But from the very beginning the Christians of Jerusalem found in the breaking of the bread which they shared, the center of the universe and the heart of their lives.

Prayers

Perhaps this refers to traditional Jewish prayer particularly the Psalms which immediately found their way into the life of the Church. But we should also think about all the indications of *Acts* noting spontaneous prayer of the community or of a person, that that be to call for God's help or to give him thanks. Between the Ascension and Pentecost (*1:4*), before a decisive election (*1:24,6:6; 13:3*), for brothers who were threatened or persecuted (*4:24-30; 6:4*) or simply to give thanks (*16:25*). Individual prayer is rarely mentioned but we feel in all these cases to what point the assembled community experiences the need of prolonging its prayer or to sing its thanksgiving. Without abandoning this custom, the whole church gives itself to prayer under the most spontaneous and direct forms.

CHAPTER XXVI
THE GOSPEL OF JESUS AND THE ACTS OF THE APOSTLES

As all know, it was the same author who wrote the third Gospel and Book of *Acts*. That author was Luke, the friend and disciple of Paul the Apostle (*Philippians 2:4; Colossians 4:14*). The two works are complementary and they complete each other. But they are very different as to subject, method and style. This difference can help us to appreciate the Christian experience at its birth and what the church meant for the first Christians.

The Gospels and above all that of Luke aim at describing the doings of Jesus from his birth to this elevation to the glory of God. In *Luke* the recital of the infant narratives and the apparition of the resurrected one gives us an image which he makes complete and makes Jesus appear in a real continuity from the banal humanity of his birth to the unique glory of his perfection. But if Luke assembles diverse and independent recitals he sets them into a global perspective of the person and work of Jesus.

In contrast, the title of the Acts is a plurality of apostles. Stephen, Peter and Paul each have their cycle and the work at least in part builds on the relationship between these three personages. This is done to put in the light, from its birth, the complexity of Christian development. Stephen opens a way for the church to adapt its style and habits in the presence of newly baptized ("Hellenists"). Paul demands that Jerusalem open its eyes as to what is happening in Antioch and Corinth. Shall we say that Jesus was not interested in these problems? Or that he forgot or was not interested in them? We simply must understand that that was not his affair and by obligating his disciples to take up their responsibility, he perfects his work.

By making *Acts* the second book following the Gospel, Luke makes an audacious initiative. He holds that the two books have as their object the same history, the same reality, namely, that the

Jesus on the way to Damascus is identical to the Jesus of Capharnum and Emmaus. He pursues the same action, assured of the same victory. But the two forms which he assumed demand two ways of writing history. That of the *Acts* is not that of the Gospel.

The gospels of course are not the work of Jesus himself but the transmission of a complexity of witnesses who were more or less eyewitnesses, redactors and codists more or less independent of each other. The source is unique: the person of Jesus but the channels which recount him are diverse. Inversely, the writing of Paul comes from his hand. But however personal is his work, no matter how important he thinks his teaching is, he never really has a point of departure. Paul can offer himself as a model and with a desire to be imitated (*I Thesalonians 1:6; I Corinthians 4:16*); but in spite of this he is only a link in a chain in a tradition which he himself received and hands on (*tradidomi*).

The *Acts* represents a departure in relation to Paul. Not only does Luke appear to ignore Paul's correspondence but he passes over in silence those points which preoccupied Paul. The only theme really common to the letters and to *Acts* is that of relation between Christians from Jewish origin and converts coming from the pagan world. And if the major themes - the baptism and the supper of the Lord - are presented from both sides and suppose the same faith, the recital of Luke appears to be ignorant of the reflections of Paul and his teaching which he draws for Jews and pagans. Is this a willed distance? How is it that Luke mentions so many details about the voyage of Paul and at the same time he is so silent on the essential points of Paul's teaching yet he is precise on details? This demands an explanation.

The simplest explanation is in the intention of Luke in composing *Acts*. In the few lines that open his second book and recalls the preface of the Gospel (*Luke 1:1-4; Acts 1:1*) the author leaves

108

us to suppose that he composed the second on the model of the first. If the facts are different, above all if the person of Jesus seems to be totally transformed, Luke holds *strongly as a base value the continuity of the episodes*. He cannot evidently read in the same way the remembrances which come from the words and acts of Jesus and the documents or recitals gathered in the church which he visits. Yet he strongly desires to put forward the unity of the event and describes it in the same style.

It has often been noted how the disappearance of Peter freed from prison recalled the happenings of Christ liberated from death, escaping the eyes of his enemies and of his disciples (*Acts 12:17-18*). Paul himself before the ancients of Ephesus puts in parallel his mission and the sufferings which await him - with the life and passion of Jesus (*Acts 20:22-24; 21:12-14*).

In the very clear examples of Peter and Paul we must add that of Stephen. The disciple who was stoned relives if not the direct kind of punishment of Jesus but at least in his way of suffering: "You will see the heavens open and the Son of Man seated at the right of the power of God" (*Luke 22:69; Acts 7:56*). The clothing confided to Saul (*7:55*) conjures up the clothing of Jesus by the soldiers (*Luke 23:24*) and his last words (*Acts 7:60*) rejoins the pardon asked by Jesus for his persecutors (*Luke 23:34*).

Acts therefore groups three persons: Peter, Paul and Stephen whose destiny reproduces more or less directly but always plainly, the passion of Jesus. These similarities suggest others as well. All three provoke their end by their severe declarations against the Judaism lived around them. All three converge on the last hours of Jesus.

By letting his recital of Paul at Rome be open as to his destiny, Luke leaves that in relation to the finality of the passion. The church remains awaiting Jesus at all times: *Maranatha, Come Lord Jesus (I Corinthians 16:22)*

CHAPTER XXVII
ETERNITY: THE ETERNAL BORE?

I have always been intrigued by the phrase in *I Corinthians 13:13* "these are things that remain - faith, hope and love and the greatest of these is love."

Theologically, there is no greater testimony to charity because, simply, God is love, charity along with *I John 4:8* where it is spelled out clearly. God does not have charity as a kind of characteristic or quality. God's nature, his substance, what God is, is love which should turn our whole notion of God upside down. This was the constant teaching of Jesus: God being love, he desires the salvation of all; he seeks the lost sheep, the prodigal son, the lost coin; he rejoices at the conversion of a sinner; that he gives life to all which is another word for love and desires not the death of the sinner (non life, non love). This was the great revelation of Jesus, that God is "Abba", life, love, forgiveness, suffering in and by his only begotten Son. Therefore that love remains forever is a foregone conclusion because that is the very nature of God. What then is eternal life as we confess it in the Creed? It is to grow forever in this love in communion with God. Since God is an infinite love, we look forward to an eternity of growth in love of God and of all God's creatures, particularly our brothers and sisters who died loving God.

This basic revelation of Jesus should also shed light on the redemptive act of Jesus. One philosopher once said that he could never believe in a father who would kill his own son to requite his own vindictiveness or disturbed sense of justice. I agree. The redemptive act of Christ is one which is freely given, whereby Christ freely gives himself over to the violence and hatred of men, returns only love and forgiveness and absorbing all hatred/violence into his being even to death, putting it to death in his sacrifice and God's 'yes' to this total gift of self and of love of all mankind in the resurrection. The redemptive act of Christ must be seen within a context of love of God for all men.

All this is so inordinately beautiful, so awesome to contemplate that "eye has not seen nor ear has heard those things God has stored up for those who love him." We are already sons of God but as yet we do not know what we will be. The only thing we *do* know is that whatever is in store for us is in the nature of love and its growth within us, for us, to us in an intimate relationship with God. That is a future which is at once known and unknown. *Known* because of the nature of God which is love; therefore all that happens and becomes of us is benevolent, loving, total self giving, unutterable. *Unknown* because God being who he is without beginning, without end, infinite in all things, we cannot begin to comprehend how God will communicate that love to and with us. We only know that he will.

At the same time, while love for the reason given is the greatest of all our virtues (they are theological because they belong directly to God), faith and hope still will remain. They are not condemned to disappear altogether. How so?

Faith is the substance of things unseen, the evidence of things hoped for. Clearly when we see God face to face, the major thrust of faith shall have been removed. But God being God, he cannot empty all that he is into the limited capacity of any creature. For that, he would have to make another God which is an oxymoron. Therefore we can receive God's love only partially into which we will grow through all eternity. We must therefore have faith in what as yet will come and hope that God through all eternity will make us grow continuously in our love for him and for each other.

Love is like a marriage which grows with the years. It matures int hat it strips away the superfluous (beauty, comeliness, organism, etc.) and goes to the core of the person where we revere, reverence and surrender to the other. The more we love the other, the less we can do without him

111

and the more he becomes part of ourselves so that we are one ever while remaining two. Something like the Trinity itself wherein each person utterly surrenders to the other, giving eternal birth to the other, being always one yet remaining in relationship as Father, Son and Spirit. One nature, three persons; one love, many persons as sons in the unique Son who is Christ becoming one in love which grows for all eternity.

Thus, the three theological virtues remain but all in a dynamic of growth, surrender, gift, unity, remaining many yet radically and always one: radical unity in the multiplicity of persons just as in the mystery of the Trinity. Viewed this way of growth in love, eternity is a constant adventure, not a repetitious bore of *deja vu*. We will continuously find new ways, new insights, new depths of this infinite love who is God. The very nature of love is absolute, i.e., it knows no limits and demands constant growth of its very nature. That is why we can say that God is love and that our relationship with him is one of love where we are joined with the eternal truth as adopted sons and daughters in the unique Son in the act of giving/receiving totally and absolutely for all eternity.

What awaits us is therefore unutterable, unimaginable and incomprehensible by us now. But we must not be afraid because we already know that whatever awaits us, is benevolent, unitive, rapturous and beyond all beauty or words to describe. As Paul says, let us console each other with these words and await the crowning of God's good work within us.

CHAPTER XXVIII
AND THE LIFE OF THE WORLD TO COME. AMEN

So many of the churches have simply given up on the whole notion of the after life. Some simply deny it altogether while some others, due to Buddhist and Eastern influence, no longer believe in a personal survival after death. Rather, they hold that we are absorbed into the one great entity-being in which there is no personal consciousness.

This view is contrary to 1600 years of recitation of the Apostles Creed. "We look forward to life everlasting. Amen." This has always been seen as a personal survival after death and not as some form of communal survival or re-incarnation in some new form of life. That is, whatever an after life can mean (and we do not really understand this fully), there is a negative and a positive aspect to this basic teaching of the Church.

Negatively, the after life is not a re-incarnation into a new life form. This is really to deny personal responsibility of a before and after. Re-incarnation may be a reward/punishment depending on the gradation of the incarnation but it is never a personal accountability for the action done during this life. There must be a before and an after, a continuum where the one before is responsible for what the one after is accountable and must pay for. The notions of heaven, hell (even purgatory) are essentially related to this concept which would be entirely destroyed by any form of re-incarnation into a new life form.

In addition, a personal absorption into a great one of the universe would also deny the same personal responsibility for acts done in this life. In fact such a concept is really related to personal nihilism where all self consciousness (of whatever nature that might be) is entirely destroyed by the very absorption into the One. Whatever Christian mysticism means, for example, no matter what images it evokes as unity ("fire hot within the fire itself") all Christian mystics have kept the distinction clearly between creature and Creator which distinction is supremely important for conserving the Christian doctrine of a personal survival after death.

Positively speaking, we must be careful in speaking of this radical transformation after death which is nothing like we have in this life. As Bossuet once put it, some Christians conceive the after life as simply switching horses and riding on again! We simply do not understand the nature of this spiritual body (which is really unknown to us) which is ours. The only thing we do know is that there is a continuum between the personal self consciousness which we have had in this life and the personal self consciousness which will be ours in the spiritual existence of the life after death with God. What this will consist in we do not know. We know that it will be the same "ego" here on earth transformed and by which we will and can recognize others who were our brothers and sisters here on earth in a union of love in God and through God, who is love itself. That self consciousness is a relationship of love between the "me", God and all those who died loving God.

We know this in the teaching of Scripture itself which holds a direct responsibility for actions done in this life on how we will be treated in the next (see *Matthew 25:31-46*). The citations are too numerous throughout the New Testament to cite them all here (e.g. see the parable of Dives, the rich man and Lazarus, the poor man). Christ explicitly tells the disciples that he will see them again after his death which he fulfills in the resurrection narratives.

But the central core of this teaching of personal survival after death lies in the very example of Jesus himself. The Gospels and the *Acts* both emphasize that it is the same Jesus both before his crucifixion and after. ("He showed them his hands and his side.") When he appears to the disciples, he shows them his hands and his side. That is, the resurrected Christ is the same one who was crucified and who walked and talked with them during his earthly period. Luke constructs both his

114

Gospel and *Acts* to show this co-relationship so that it is the same Jesus, not a ghost or a phantom, that appears to Paul on his way to Damascus as it was the same Jesus who taught in Capharnum and Jerusalem. This is a core teaching of the Gospels and of the entire New Testament. If therefore the Master is the same both before and after death, the disciples who will be with Christ after death will be the same as well as to personal consciousness. This core teaching applies to the disciples as well since Christ is first from among the dead, so too the rest will follow in their own turn.

Once again, we do not know what that condition in the next life will be like. "Eye has not seen and ear has not heard the things that God has reserved for those who love him." But whatever that condition, it will be us, each of us, who will relate to God and to each other forever in love, because as we learn from Scripture, God is love as the very definition of his very being.

CHAPTER XXIX
GOD NEEDS US TO LOVE : *John 15:9-17*

The great revelation presented in the ancient covenant and given in the new as the last word of the truth of God and of man and which establishes every being in its existence and leads it to its perfection, is love.

I John 4;7-10 intimately relates love and knowledge: to know God and to love God are mutually interdependent. "To know" in the Bible serves to designate the sexual union of a man and woman, therefore and integral sharing of intimacy. The only one who knows perfectly is the one who loves. By love, we are not external neither to God not to the neighbor because the love of God is totally lived by love of the neighbor. By accepting to love the neighbor, that is, making and placing ourselves at his service as Christ did for us, we become capable of understanding that God is love.

This is the capital and essential revelation of the whole New Testament whereas most of us view God as a terrible despot, stern judge of our least faults.

Christ says "I have loved you as the Father has loved me" (*John 15:9*). That small word "as" is phenomenal. It establishes an equivalence between the love of the Father for Christ and the love of Christ for us. That truly is amazing. We can translate as follows: the love of the Father for us passes by Christ because we are all in a certain sense contained in the humanity of Christ. This love is diffused. We can remain in this love only by keeping the commandments given by Jesus just as he kept the commandments of his Father. All these commandments are summed up in one: to love as Christ has loved us. We have the impression of a constant circulation of love but is love not anything else but the circulation of life? We come to an astonishing conclusion: every time that we love, it is God himself *who loves in us and by us because God loves us by others*. Sin consists in

116

blocking this circulation/passage of love of God as if, refusing to love, we impede God from loving our brothers and sisters. That is blasphemy on our part, the quintessential sin. Is it possible for us to love others as God loves, with the very same love which comes from God and who is God? Yes! We have received the Spirit, we *have* received that love that empowers us to love as God loves in the Holy Spirit.

A servant really does not know what his master does. That is why he is servant. Thus the theme of knowledge once again. The servant obeys his master because he does not know himself by himself what is good. This clearly is an allusion to the time of the law: if there is law it is because there is ignorance of good and evil and we obey for the simple reason that we are commanded and we are ignorant of what is truly good and evil. With Christ we have exited the time of ignorance because, he says, "all that I have learned from my Father, I have made it known to you." We have entered now into knowledge and in love because to know is to love and what is to be human is precisely that love as the foundation of everything. Jesus can now call us "friends" because we are one with him in both knowledge and love. Nothing more remains to do except what Christ did. "Go and bear fruit." Jesus has gone before us. The fruit that he brings forth, it is us reborn by and in love.

II.

To love is therefore to risk, to risk being broken, deceived, abandoned. That is why most people refuse to commit to love because it is so dangerous and devastating, if lost or deceived.

John ends the first conclusion of his Gospel (the second conclusion is Chapter 21) by saying that the facts and actions of Christ were narrated in his Gospel that we may believe in Jesus and by believing in Christ, we may have life in his name. There is a new birth, a re-finding of life. We must become conscious of the consequences for us of the resurrection of Christ. When Jesus rose from the dead, it is we who, by him and with him, rise from the dead. Pious discourse? Empty language? To go beyond cliches, we must understand what that means and what it demands. By the resurrection of Christ we have received a profound revelation: that God is love through and through. Easter is a sort of demonstration, of a proclamation destined for all men and women. We learn that God, the foundation of all that is, the truth of man, is love and consequently, life is given to us freely as Jesus gave us his life freely and willingly.

But Easter is not just a demonstration; it is also an appeal, a calling. An appeal to love, an appeal to do what Christ did in memory always of Christ. Yet this must pass by faith. Faith in Christ to that which Easter represents, the perfection of life itself. Clearly this faith is itself a gift, a given, but we must accept to receive it which is presented as a trial which is so beautifully narrated for us in the story of Thomas, the Apostle. Like him, we know of the resurrection of Christ only by testimony, by living witnesses. We must believe on the word. Therefore, Thomas is our turn, even if Jesus ceded to Thomas his desire to see and to touch. This desire of Thomas is also our desire as well but it will be satisfied only later because the route traveled by Thomas in this Gospel designates and describes the map of our whole life. In waiting to encounter Christ, we are under the regime of

118

"believing without seeing." Paul said it best: "faith comes from hearing" (*Romans 10:17*). *Seeing gives us a knowledge not a believing.* Only hearing puts us in relation with him from whom we receive the Word. Seeing leaves us on the outside. Only hearing lets us in because it is received only in faith.

It is because we believe in the love manifested by Christ giving and taking up his life again for us *that we can risk to love.* Our love must be and is an echo of his love. As John put it, God has loved us first (*I John 5:1-6*). This is surprising because John gives this love in the form of a commandment. That is because love cannot be facultative: who does not love is not born of God, that is, we are not the image and likeness of the one who has created and founded us. To be image and likeness comes back to being created, to exist, to escape our nothingness (*Genesis 1:27*). And this cannot be done without our consent and freedom. However, it is not for us a simple question of imitation of God as Christ has revealed him: we are absolutely incapable of loving as God loves by the efforts of our will or by any work of ours. That is why Easter is not content to give us an example: it gives us a sacred force, a dynamic force to bring this about, the Spirit of God himself who is love who inhabits our hearts. Easter is accomplished in us only by Pentecost.

EPILOGUE

I have tried to give the reader the fruit of my years of prayer and meditation on the central mystery of our sacred faith which is the life-death-resurrection of Jesus along with some entailments of that pascal mystery. I hope that I have met with some success in doing so.

These mysteries are precisely that - beyond rational comprehension, beyond the powers of our minds to fathom and to understand. But then understanding cannot be our primary goal since we deal here with mystery and not because we are too stupid to understand but because these mysteries come from the heart of God revealed to us in and through the mystery of the incarnation. Only God can speak of God, only God can reveal to us his very essence of who and what he is *for us*. And that is au we need to know. They are mystery in the sense that they cannot be deciphered from the world, they must be said by the world and that this truth is accessible only through faith.

For the rest all we need to know is that this mystery is terribly good news for us, that God loves us and wants to be one with us now here on earth and through all eternity. That gives us utter joy even amidst the sufferings and inevitable death in our lives and in the lives of those whom we hold near and dear. No matter what the pain and agony, victory is ours even amidst the greatest suffering in our lives. While we can never be free of the pain of our existence, the one thing which the good news assures us is peace, the peace of Christ given in the Holy Spirit who is spread forth in our hearts making us the one body of Jesus Christ on earth as it is in heaven.

It is on that note of joy that I wish to end this book, a joy that I wish for you, unknown to me but whom I already love in the mystical body of Jesus Christ. Then in that eternal kingdom we shall know each other, love each other in ways which eye has not seen nor ear heard of the great things that God has stored up for those who love him. I pray fervently and with all my heart that all of us be saved and meet in that blessed eternity with the Father, the Son and the Holy Spirit.

Peter J. Riga is an attorney practicing appellate law in Houston, Texas. He is a writer of over thirty five books and over five thousand articles on law, foreign and domestic affairs, foreign policy, ethics, philosophy, theology and scripture as well as comparative religions including Islam. Mr. Riga has three doctorates in philosophy, theology and law. He was a former chaplain in Vietnam with the 101 st Airborne Division and received the bronze star and purple heart. He was a missionary and parish pastor along with other ecclesial offices. He taught law and theology at various universities including the University of Florida, University of California at Berkeley and South Texas College of Law. He studied as well in universities in Europe. This rich background gives him great insights into the present study of Islam war on Christians throughout the Islamic world.

Other books by Peter Riga at AuthorHouse include:

Our Death Struggle With Islam 2006
The Nature of Evil 2003
All You Wanted To Know About Islam And Didn't Know Where To Look 2002
The Passion and Death of Christ 2004

Peter Riga may be contacted at
PeterRiga@gmail.com and P.O. Box 52518, Houston, TX 77052